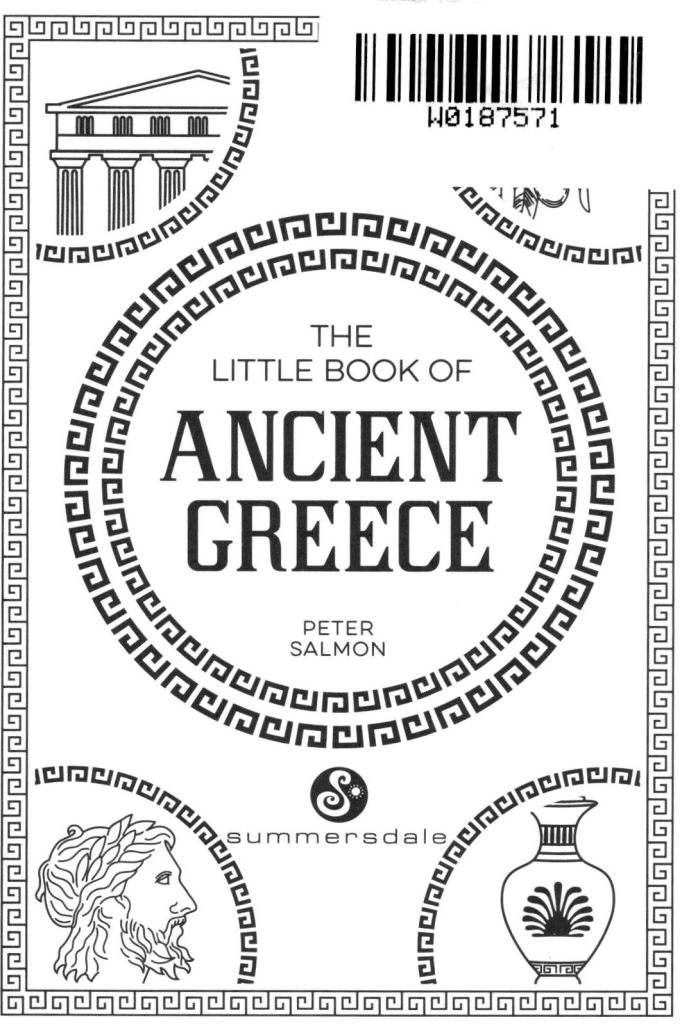

THE
LITTLE BOOK OF
ANCIENT GREECE

PETER SALMON

summersdale

THE LITTLE BOOK OF ANCIENT GREECE

An Hachette UK Company
www.hachette.co.uk

Summersdale Publishers
Part of Octopus Publishing Group Limited
Carmelite House
50 Victoria Embankment
LONDON
EC4Y 0DZ
UK

www.summersdale.com

The authorized representative in the EEA is Hachette Ireland, 8 Castlecourt Centre, Dublin 15, D15 XTP3, Ireland (email: info@hbgi.ie)

Printed and bound in Poland

ISBN: 978-1-83799-535-6
eISBN: 978-1-83799-536-3

This FSC® label means that materials and other controlled sources used for the product have been responsibly sourced

	MIX
FSC	Papper | Bidrar till ansvarsfullt skogsbruk
www.fsc.org	FSC® C018236

Substantial discounts on bulk quantities of Summersdale books are available to corporations, professional associations and other organizations. For details contact general enquiries: telephone: +44 (0) 1243 771107 or email: enquiries@summersdale.com.

CONTENTS

INTRODUCTION

Sometime between 450 and 420 BCE, a man from Halicarnassus took up his pen and started work on a new sort of book. His name was Herodotus, and he wanted "to preserve the fame of the important and remarkable achievements produced by both Greeks and non-Greeks". To do this, he created a completely new type of narrative: a history.

Herodotus seems to have realized that there was something incredibly special about Greek civilization. In fact, some would argue it is the greatest civilization of all time, cradle not only of history, but philosophy, mathematics, astronomy, law, chemistry, medicine, theatre, poetry, biology and sculpture. We even have the Greeks to thank for democracy, alarm clocks, cheesecake and the Olympics!

This book takes us on a thrilling journey into the glorious past that was Ancient Greece – from inside the mind of Socrates, to inside the warships of Alexander the Great. Along the way we'll meet some of the greatest writers, statesmen, warriors and scientists of all time, and discover that the world we live in now is one that owes a huge debt to a group of people who first arrived on the human stage over 3,000 years ago...

AN INTRODUCTION TO ANCIENT GREECE

Ancient Greece continues, thousands of years later, to fascinate us, inspire us, and to inform our everyday lives. The Ancient Greeks are a reference point for so much of our Western world. But who were they, what did they do, and how is it that what was a small country on the Mediterranean would grow to be one of the greatest empires the world has known?

Come on a journey into a past which astonishes not just for what it is, but in how familiar much of it is – because what happened there during that time affects, in so many ways, what is happening here now.

THE CRADLE OF WESTERN CIVILIZATION

Ancient Greece has long been known as the "cradle of Western civilization". When Herodotus took up his pen, Ancient Greece had been established for around 800 years, and it would continue for almost 500 more. In the course of its 1,300 years, it would, as we shall see, produce some of the greatest thinkers, and some of the greatest warriors, in human history.

At its peak in the fourth century BCE, 8–10 million people would have regarded themselves as being ruled by Greece, which was nearly a quarter of the world's population. And its empire covered some 2 million square miles, from what we now know as Russia and Ukraine on the eastern borders, all the way to Spain in the west.

But it has never just been about size when it comes to Ancient Greece. Other empires have dwarfed it in terms of population and acreage. But none have come close to its influence. In fact, the book you are holding in your hands is part of a long history of telling the Greeks' story – a story which started with the most beautiful woman in the world.

THE MOST BEAUTIFUL WOMAN IN THE WORLD

Her name was Helen, and some believe she was the daughter of the god Zeus, and Leda, the wife of a king from the Greek city of Sparta. Paris – a prince from the city of Troy – had been promised the most beautiful woman in the world by the goddess Aphrodite. So, one day, he kidnapped Helen and took her to Troy. The Greeks raised a fleet to go and get her back, and this made her "the face that launched a thousand ships".

The war over Helen – the Trojan War – would go down in legend, but more than that, it would go down in poetry. The bard Homer told the story of the last ten days of the battle to reclaim Helen in *The Iliad*, and then the story of the journey home of the Greek hero Odysseus in *The Odyssey*.

Was there a Trojan War? Debates continue. But those who believe there was place it at a date of around 1200 BCE. Whether or not Homer had his facts right and Ancient Greece began with Zeus and Leda, something shifted in the history of the world at around that date.

THE TROJAN WAR

It is, in many ways, the founding myth of the Greeks – the battle of their forebears, the Achaeans as Homer called them, against the city of Troy, to bring Helen home after Paris abducted her. The war is said to have lasted ten years, and many of the events have passed into our own history and language.

For example, the Trojan Horse, and the expression "beware of Greeks bearing gifts", which refers to the large wooden horse the Achaeans left outside the gates of Troy. The Trojans took it inside, believing it to be a victory gift. Then, when night fell, the horse opened and Greek soldiers poured out, opened the gates to allow their army in, and defeated Troy. They reclaimed Helen, and the hero of the Trojans, Hector, was killed and dragged around the city behind a chariot – a profound display of contempt.

We have only the Homeric myths, and the poems of later Romans such as Virgil, to tell us of the war's existence. A founding myth tells us what a nation wants to be. The Greeks saw themselves as a heroic race, and so it would prove.

HOMER

Some 2,800 years after his death, Homer is still regarded as one of the greatest authors in history. His two epic poems, *The Iliad*, which tells the story of the Trojan War, and *The Odyssey*, which tells the adventures of one of its soldiers, Odysseus, continue to yield new translations and adaptations, everything from *Ulysses* by James Joyce to the film *O Brother, Where Art Thou?* by the Coen brothers.

Of the man himself, we know very little. In fact, scholars are divided over whether he was the author of both texts – or even of one of them! Many see the name "Homer" as a label for a group of poets whose work evolved over centuries. Perhaps Homer is the name of the man who edited the final versions – one meaning attributed to Homer is "he who fits (the song) together".

The Ancient Greeks seemed sure that the poet was one man, and that the two books are works of genius. We may not agree on the first point, but it is impossible to disagree with the second.

THE DARK AGES

The Greek Dark Ages, which historians refer to as the time between 1200 and 800 BCE, displayed little of the intellectual and artistic glory we have come to associate with Ancient Greece. There were, as far as we know, no Homers, no Platos, no Aristotles, no Euclids and no Sapphos – each of whom, as we shall see, produced some of the greatest works of humankind.

However, as the Iron Age began to take shape between 1200 and 500 BCE, these Greeks were at the forefront of changes in technology, such as new weapons and ceramics. Moving into the space left by the fall of the Mycenaean Greeks (1750–1050 BCE), who had met their end either in an earthquake or a war, the new Greeks built on their predecessors' achievements.

There was little to suggest that these new inhabitants of Greece would become the Ancient Greeks as we have come to know them. But one invention, partly their own, partly borrowed, was to begin a process that would come to dominate the world.

THE WRITTEN WORD

When Homer told his tales of Helen and the Trojan War, and of Odysseus battling the Cyclops and the Sirens, he would have done so by an age-old method: oral transmission. Many of the formulaic techniques used by the poet, such as repetition and verses, were to help the reciter remember the huge texts – each of which ran to thousands of verses.

Then, somewhere around 800 BCE, Greece rediscovered a lost art: writing. We have some Greek writing from before 1300 BCE, but nothing then for 500 years – hence the name the Dark Ages. Taking the idea of writing from neighbouring Phoenicia (now regarded as the eastern Mediterranean and Lebanon), and adding what we would call vowels, the Greek alphabet suddenly transformed the culture.

Now poets didn't need to remember so many words, which doubtless came as a relief. But more importantly, the written word altered the way Ancient Greeks thought – with repercussions that are still being felt in disciplines such as philosophy and politics. It is no exaggeration to say this is the birthplace of the Western mind as we know it.

THE ARCHAIC PERIOD

Unfortunately for historians, historical eras don't start on the dot – there is always a period of transition and, after all, the era is usually named well after it occurs. Who knows what historians in three thousand years will call our own time!

That said, when dealing with Ancient Greece, it is conventional to refer to the Dark Ages ending, and what is known as the Archaic period beginning, in exactly 800 BCE. Greeks went to bed at midnight at the end of 801 BCE swathed in darkness, and woke, if not quite swathed in light, then swathed in the archaic. Little did they know that they had begun a journey different from that of any other civilization before them, and that a mere 320 years later, their descendants would be part of the greatest flowering of human knowledge ever. These ancestors would go to bed archaic and wake up classical.

NUMBERS GAME

"Archaic" is, in fact, a word from the Greek, from *arkhaios*, meaning "ancient, old-fashioned, antiquated, primitive". Of course, archaic people don't really know they are archaic, so using the word is an anachronism – which is another word from the Greek, meaning "a chronological inconsistency" (*ana* meaning "backwards", and *khronos* meaning "time"). As you can see, once the Greeks started writing things down, they gifted us a lot of words!

For all their achievements, the Archaic Greeks lacked a lot of things which were required for the Classical era to begin, and first among these was a sufficiently large population. If you are going to change the world, you need people on the ground, and in 800 BCE Greece there were only about 700,000 people, roughly the same as Luxembourg today. (No offence to Luxembourg, but it seems unlikely to change Western civilization quite as radically as the Ancient Greeks did!)

By 350 BCE that number had increased to around 10 million – more than ten times as many in just 450 years. By then, one tenth of the Earth's population was Greek. Where did they all come from? And what were they doing?

KEEPING ACCOUNT

One answer is that they came from other places. There was a great deal of immigration to mainland Greece, as developments in agriculture and politics fed population growth, and population growth fed developments in agriculture and politics.

Trade was also growing. Then (as now) Greece was known for its olives, its wine and its pottery. It was also at the forefront of metalwork, particularly bronze. Money started to flow into Greece.

Fortunately, one of Ancient Greece's main imports has ceased to be traded: slaves. But food staples, spices, wood and metal are part of any healthy economy, and the Archaic Greeks were no slouches in bringing them in. With all of this activity, new business practices also came in, which we can still recognize today – taxation, tariffs and coins.

There was also huge trade in papyrus – writing really had caught on, and accounts needed to be kept, transactions recorded, invoices sent out.

But if people were flowing into Greece, they were also flowing out. They were not emigrating; they were setting up colonies. As Herodotus noted in his *The Histories*, the empire had slowly begun.

HERODOTUS

The "father of history", Herodotus was born in what is now Turkey, in 484 BCE. He spent much of his early life travelling, and would draw on these adventures when he came to write his *The Histories*. As much as his book is a story of kings, queens and generals, and of famous battles and tragedies, it is also a marvellous collection of myths and legends, tall stories and travellers' tales.

He is a storyteller as much as a historian. He always prefers a bad joke to no joke at all, and would rather tell a story and let us decide if it is true, than check the facts himself. In Libya, we are told, there are giant snakes, dog-headed men and headless men with eyes in their breasts ("I merely repeat what the Libyans say," he writes), while in India there is a bird "so strong that it can take up an elephant in its talons" and ants that dig up gold.

As he himself put it, "Very few things happen at the right time, and the rest do not happen at all. The conscientious historian will correct these defects."

SETTLEMENTS

While the Greek mainland would always remain the centre of the Greek empire, the Archaic era saw the first waves of expansion which would eventually bring a huge proportion of the globe under the control of the Greeks.

Some of this was through the establishment of settlements. There were two types of settlement. The first was known as *emporia*, from which we get the word "emporium" – and yes, these were a type of shopping centre, or at least trading posts where goods could be manufactured and exchanged. They spread across the Mediterranean, the Sea of Marmara (in what is now Turkey) and the Black Sea.

More important were the settlements which later became independent cities of Greece, spreading across Europe and into the Balkans. The first of these was set up in Sicily, and soon after in places like Marseille (in modern France) and Cyrene (in modern Libya).

In fact, there were so many settlements in southern Italy that it became known as Magna Graecia – Greater Greece!

BUILDING AN EMPIRE

There was also, of course, what historians have called the "shotgun method" – colonisation, pure and simple. As in the history of any empire, independent populations were invaded, rebels killed, and the empire given dominion. This would reach its height under Alexander the Great 150 years later, but it began in Archaic Greece.

By the end of the sixth century BCE, the population of the Greek mainland had grown to 3 million, while the population of the Greek settlements outside the mainland accounted for another 2 million. Of the 10 million Greeks in 350 BCE, around 6 million were outside the mainland.

This, of course, brought its own problems: how does one run an empire? There are plenty of examples in history of ruling tyrants and despots, but the Greeks were developing new methods of governance. In the Archaic period, we see the first hints at what would become the sort of political systems that exist today. First among these was the development of the very thing we get the word "political" from: the *polis*, meaning "city". And the man who takes the credit was a poet, named Solon.

SOLON

He became known as one of the Seven Sages of Greece, but Solon's origins are obscure. We do know that he was about 30 when he came to public prominence in 600 BCE, reciting one of his poems which roused the Athenians to win a war that seemed lost. But it was not through poetry that Solon acquired his fame.

His fame came not from revolution but reform. Made *archon* (essentially, a governor) in 594, he instituted the sort of government that is recognizable today. His initial popularity was based on what was known as the *seisachtheia*, meaning "the shaking off of burdens". This involved debt relief, the freeing of slaves, and the return of lands taken by the aristocracy.

He also strengthened the idea of the *polis* – the idea of a community working together – so he began forming cities out of villages that were close to each other. This form of urbanization made the population stronger and more dynamic. His system of laws would become a model for all later democratic societies.

He died aged 80, and was celebrated for that most Greek of virtues: moderation.

SPARTA

But Athens didn't have the Archaic period to itself. In fact, while Solon was transforming his city-state, nearby Sparta was widely recognized as the leading Greek state. Legend has it the state grew in prominence 60 years after the Trojan War, when the area was invaded by a people known as the Dorians.

Sparta had a Dark Age, and it too had a legendary figure who led them out of it: Lycurgus, which means "wolf". As Solon did with Athens, Lycurgus brought law and order, and a stable political and economic state. He also incorporated nearby city-states into Sparta, either by treaty or force, a practice that continued after his death.

This became known as the Peloponnesian League, after the city of Peloponnese, and included legendary cities such as Corinth, Argos and Megalopolis, which literally means "massive city" – legend has it that giants lived there at one time!

There was also a city that was to find fame for a different reason. Its name was Olympia and in 776 BCE, it gathered together the best warriors and athletes in all of Greece, and held a series of games.

THE OLYMPIC GAMES

Olympia was named after Mount Olympus, the home of the gods, and the athletes came from everywhere to compete – from as far west as Spain, and as far east as the Black Sea. To qualify, participants had to be "legitimate sons of free-born Greek parents". As with so many things in Ancient Greece, only men were allowed to compete.

Many of the sports are recognizable, like running, wrestling, long jump, shot put, javelin, boxing and equestrian events. And while we don't have the medal count, or a list of winners, we do know that a cook from the city of Elis, named Koroibos, won a 600-feet long foot race.

Did everyone compete in the nude, as rumour has it? Accounts vary. In fact, one legend has it that it was Koroibos who kicked things off, after his shorts fell off while racing, and others followed his example!

The Olympics was held every four years for over 800 years, until 393 CE, long after the fall of Greece. They would not be held again until 1896, in Athens. No one was nude on that occasion, a tradition that thankfully continues to this day...

SLAVES

But it wasn't just athletes and warriors who were carrying out physical tasks at this time. The Greek empire was built on many things, but one of the main ones was slavery. It is difficult to know the exact number of slaves in Greece at any one time, but an estimate in the *Encyclopaedia Britannica* puts the figure at close to a third of the Greek population when Greece was in its pomp.

Some of these slaves were the spoils of war, others were part of a huge slave trade. In Greece, most were "employed" in agriculture, while others were set to work silver mining. These mines were the source of much of the wealth of Athens, and the use of free labour in dangerous conditions was especially beneficial to those in positions of power.

Closer to home, household slaves were common in wealthy families, the males taking on roles such as farming in times of peace and personal servants in times of war. Female slaves were used for domestic tasks.

Greece would become famous for its intellectual culture. Might we argue that you have a lot more time to think if a slave is taking care of all the hard work?

THE HOME OF THE GODS

The names are familiar to us: Zeus, Aphrodite, Apollo, Dionysus, Poseidon, Athena. With their home atop Mount Olympus, Greek gods and goddesses were central to Greek life and were believed to guide the fate of each individual, and of nations. Offend a god, and life would take a turn for the worse – and if your life had taken a turn for the worse, then you must have done something to offend.

This meant a lot of praising the gods and offering them sacrifices. If you were to take to the sea, best appease the god of the sea, Poseidon, before setting out. If you wanted a good harvest, then pay homage to Demeter, goddess of agriculture.

But don't fall into the trap of *hubris* – a Greek word meaning "excessive pride towards or defiance of the gods" – or *nemesis*, your "downfall", is sure to follow. The gods are, in Greek religion, a capricious lot. You can never be quite sure what they will do next, and they are not above acting with spite for no reason. Maybe they still operate? Or does everything in the world seem rational to you?

THE IONIAN REVOLT

In 499 BCE, a number of Greek cities in Ionia (modern-day Turkey), which had fallen under Persian control half a century earlier, revolted against the invaders. The rest of Greece rushed to their aid. Persia, under Darius the Great, immediately struck back, reclaiming the Ionian cities. By 493 the Ionian revolt had been put down. But this was not the end of something, it was the beginning – of the Greco-Persian wars, and of Classical Greece.

Of course, those living at the time did not know it, but later historians would name the Ionian revolt as the beginning of one of the greatest flowerings of Western civilization. Between 499 BCE and the death of Alexander the Great in 323 BCE, Greece would transform itself, and transform us, in ways that those on the front line of the war against Persia could not have imagined. Art, politics, literature, philosophy, law and religion, to name only a small fraction of the things Classical Greece would change forever, were very different when Alexander died.

THE GRECO-PERSIAN WARS: PART ONE

For the next 50 years, Greece and Persia would fight a series of battles that have gone down in history. The Battle of Marathon. The Battle of Salamis. The Battle of Plataea. Legends were made, and the Western world reshaped.

It was Darius the Great of Persia who attacked first in 490 BCE, winning a series of victories and verbally attacking Athens. But the Persians were defeated at the Battle of Marathon, famous for the efforts of one man, Pheidippides, who saw some Persian ships break away and head towards Athens. He ran 26 miles from Marathon to the capital to tell the rulers the ships were coming – it is from this legend we get the name of the race "the marathon", and its distance.

Ten years later, with Darius dead, his son Xerxes took up the fight. Attacking in 480 BCE, Xerxes' declared aim was to take all of Greece. Had he succeeded, the world would be very different. But, despite hugely superior numbers, his invading force soon found itself running aground on the Greek courage that became legendary. At Thermopylae he met, head on, Leonidas from Sparta.

LEONIDAS

The Greco-Persian wars saw many famous conflicts, and one that has passed into legend is the Battle of Thermopylae, in which a mere 7,000 Greeks faced up to 300,000 Persians. A Greek victory looked impossible, but the Greeks held out for seven days, a decisive delay which allowed their forces to regroup and eventually win the war.

There were many heroes, but greatest of all was Leonidas. Born in 540 BCE, he had risen to become the king of Sparta in 489 BCE. Nine years later, he and his Spartan army – we get our word "Spartan", meaning "marked by simplicity, frugality, or avoidance of luxury and comfort" from the reputation they built under Leonidas – defended the pass of Thermopylae in central Greece. There they fought overwhelming odds. All died, Leonidas included, but all passed into legend for their bravery and self-sacrifice.

Leonidas became the subject of epics and poems, and statues were raised to him across Greece. His final command echoes down the centuries: "Never surrender!"

THE GRECO-PERSIAN WARS: PART TWO

Despite the setbacks, Persia continued to attack, and Greece continued to defend. The fall of Thermopylae, whatever the costs, made Xerxes confident he could press on to Athens. His chosen point of attack was the straits between the mainland and Salamis, an island in the Saronic Gulf near Athens. It was to be the largest naval battle in ancient history and is generally regarded as a turning point in the war.

The Greeks started with 370 ships; the Persians had 900. However, the Greeks knew the chaotic waters well, and in the narrow straits the sheer number of Persian ships proved a hindrance. Some 300 Persian ships were sunk, compared to 40 Greek ones. The Persians were forced to retreat.

The second Persian invasion continued for another year, before the loss of the Battle of Plataea saw Xerxes admit defeat. He withdrew to Persia, and spent the rest of his life constructing his own great cities and building his own great culture.

In Greece, war had brought the collection of city-states together as one, and they were ready to begin constructing something that would outdo Persia, or anywhere else.

ARTEMISIA I OF CARIA

The Battle of Salamis marked a turning point in Persia's invasion of Greece. Many heroes were made by the battle, but none stood as high as the queen of the city-state of Halicarnassus, Artemisia, who fought as an ally of Xerxes. Despite the fact that she fought against the Greeks, they revered her name.

When the general Themistocles encouraged Xerxes to engage in a naval fight at Salamis, Artemisia was the only one of his generals to argue against it. But once the decision was made, she showed incredible courage and tactical skill in the heat of battle. In command of five ships, she attacked relentlessly, even as defeat loomed, sinking some of the Greeks' best ships. Xerxes was moved to say, "My men have become women; and my women, men."

Legend has it she later died by suicide, jumping from the top of the Rock of Leucas, after her love for a man named Dardanus was rebuffed. But, ever the warrior, she blinded him before she did it.

CLASSICAL GREECE

Art, mathematics, politics, law, theatre, literature, philosophy and science. In Western civilization, there is a "before Greece" and an "after Greece" for all of these disciplines. The end of the Greco-Persian wars, and Greece's growing confidence, saw an intellectual rising beyond anything the world had known until that time.

So many men (and this was a very male society) would be described as "the father of" their branch of knowledge. From Socrates in philosophy and Herodotus in history, to Hippocrates in medicine, this was a time of huge intellectual change and invention.

As the historian Will Durant put it, "excepting machinery, there is hardly anything secular in our culture that does not come from Greece." He was wrong in fact – much of our machinery also comes from the Greeks. Gears. The use of steam. Screws. Bronze casting. Water mills. Showers. Central heating. Alarm clocks. Vending machines.

They also developed mining for metals, and many of our plumbing techniques come from Ancient Greece. They also invented a lot of toys, including one which has had its share of ups and downs...

YO-YOs

They may have been inventing Western civilization, but the Ancient Greeks still knew how to have fun.

For many years historians had known about a Greek toy involving a disc and a piece of string – it kept popping up in literature, but no one knew what it was. Then, a terracotta vase from 440 BCE was discovered that shows a young man in traditional Greek clothes, with one arm extended. Hanging down is a piece of string, and on the end of the string is a disc.

Here was yet another invention that the Greeks got to first: the yo-yo. In fact, it was not until 1928, over 2,000 years later, that the first yo-yos were commercially available.

Other Greek toys include marbles, jacks (made from the knucklebones of sheep and goats), draughts, baby rattles and spinning tops. They also played tug-of-war. Most artful of all were dolls, made from wax, wood, clay, stone and ivory. As part of their marriage ceremony, girls would give their dolls to their gods as a form of sacrifice.

As far as we know, they were allowed to keep their yo-yos.

PEACE

The end of the Greco-Persian wars saw peace come to Greece for the first time in several generations. It was a time of expansion into foreign lands, and into new ways of thinking. The first of the great Greek poets after Homer, a man named Pindar, was born in 518 BCE in the village of Cynoscephalae, near Thebes. Pindar is best known for his *Victory Odes*, celebrations of triumphs achieved by competitors in the Olympic Games.

An air of celebration lives in Pindar's odes, reflecting Greece's growing stature and importance. But his poems are also self-reflective about his art. It is the first stirring of a main character trait of the Greeks – they didn't just live, they reflected on how they lived, how they loved, how they fought, how they died. They even reflected on how and why they reflected – it is from this that philosophy was born.

Pindar died in 438 BCE at the age of 80. He lived through war, and perhaps believed that his children would only live through peace. He was wrong. Seven years after his death, Greece was at war again, this time with itself.

THE PELOPONNESIAN WAR

Athens and Sparta had long kept an uneasy truce. The alliance between the Delian League of Athens, and the Peloponnesian League of the Spartans allowed both to grow in strength and prestige. Having joined to fight off the Persians, however, their alliance broke down after victory.

For 30 years they avoided war, but this changed as Athens began to take more and more control of Greek affairs. Border skirmishes erupted; territory was invaded. Finally, in 431 BCE, war broke out. It was a war as epic as the Trojan War of legend. Every battle seemed to end in stalemate as the superior navy of Athens and the superior land army of Sparta drove each other to a standstill. The casualties were tremendous.

In fact, it was to take some 27 years for the war to draw to a close, with the final victory going to the Spartans under the command of their leader, Lysander, who destroyed the Athenian fleet in 405 BCE. This left the Spartans the masters of Greece. It was not a position they were to hold for long.

THUCYDIDES

The Peloponnesian War has another claim to fame: it is the first war of which we have a first-hand account, written while it was actually happening. The account was written by an Athenian general named Thucydides. And, if Herodotus is the father of history as storytelling, Thucydides has claim to be the father of history as truth telling.

Despite his rank and allegiance, Thucydides attempted something never before done in historical writing – he strove to be objective. While debates still rage about whether he managed to be so, no one doubts he made the attempt. As he put it, "I lived through the whole of it, being of an age to comprehend events, and giving my attention to them in order to know the exact truth about them."

We know little about Thucydides' life other than what we read in his history. He was Athenian; he was a general; he fought; he caught the plague, and ended up in exile, writing his history. A history which, he assures the reader, contains no fables. Unlike, he implies, that of funny old Herodotus!

ATHENS REDUX

It is one thing to win a war, another to rule an empire. The Spartans would go down in history as great warriors, fearless, relentless, unwilling to take a step back. In Lysander they had one of the greatest soldiers in history. But after their victory in 405 BCE, the Spartans proved themselves less successful as politicians, and Lysander much less successful as a ruler.

By 395 BCE, they were involved in another Greek war, this time with Thebes, which would last eight years and see them lose a great deal of influence, despite what looked like a victory. Lysander was killed in battle in 395 BCE, and those who followed were no great warriors or statesmen.

While Sparta frittered away its power on yet another war, Athens licked its wounds and began the restoration of its own empire, at the same time as instigating some of the great civil, intellectual and architectural works in its history. When Sparta signed a treaty with Persia, known as the "King's Peace", it handed over much of its power to its former enemies, and thus Athens became the great power of Classical Greece.

PERICLES

They called Pericles "the first citizen of Athens", and it was through him that Greece's capital first acquired its status as the cultural centre of the world. As a statesman, he virtually invented the idea of democracy as we still understand it today. In his quest to make Athens the first city of the empire, he started a programme of construction, and it is to him we owe the Acropolis, including the Parthenon, which remains one of the greatest achievements in architecture.

Born in around 495 BCE, he ruled Athens from 461 until his death in 429 BCE. In many ways, his Athens was the model on which all future cities would be built. A place of citizens, of business, of art and culture. His speeches were spoken calmly, but contained thunder and lightning. Militarily he was cautious but won a number of naval battles.

Much of the Acropolis still stands, in tribute to the genius of Pericles. But as he himself said, "What you leave behind is not what is engraved in stone monuments, but what is woven into the lives of others." In this he was a master craftsman.

ATHENS ASCENDANT

When people think of Ancient Greece, it is normally of the 200 years between the Ionian Revolt and the death of Alexander the Great. It is staggering the ways in which Greece grew, developed, invented, conquered and dominated. The last two centuries in the West, from the Industrial Revolution to the Technological Revolution, is perhaps the only era that compares.

The era was not without conflicts – as Athens attempted to build another league similar to the Delian League, a number of city-states revolted, but the battles failed to grow in size to all-out wars, and Athens was able to grow in influence and power. The population continued to grow as well, with Greece becoming the centre of the world for traders, businesspeople and intellectuals.

But one threat emerged in the middle of the fourth century which Athens had not foreseen. To the north a new power was emerging, which would soon become the dominant state of Ancient Greece. Its name was Macedon (commonly known now as Macedonia), and its ruler Philip II. He and his son would change Greece forever.

THE RISE OF MACEDON

Born in about 383 BCE, Philip II, the youngest son of Amyntas III, spent several years as a hostage in Thebes, where he gained a military education. Returning to Macedon in 364, within five years he had ascended to the throne, and from 359 his military skills and ambitious vision of Macedonia saw him begin to expand his kingdom.

A series of victories saw the boundaries of Macedon move ever closer to Athens, and the statesman Demosthenes urged Athenians to push back against the upstart kingdom. From around 352 to 338, Athens and Macedon were essentially at war and in 338, Philip won the decisive Battle of Chaeronea and became de facto King of Greece.

But it wasn't enough for him. He decided to push into Asia Minor, which roughly equates to what is now Turkey. Greek cities on the western coast welcomed his armies and joined in attempts to overthrow the ruling Achaemenids.

But in October 336 BCE, Philip was assassinated by one of his own bodyguards while attending a wedding. His son Alexander ascended to the throne. He was to make his father's astonishing achievements seem small fry.

ALEXANDER THE GREAT

Alexander became king at the age of 20, and by the age of 30 he had conquered much of Asia and Egypt, adding them to his European kingdom, and making his Greece one of the greatest empires the world has known. Never defeated in battle, even when outnumbered, Alexander the Great is still regarded as perhaps the greatest military genius of all time.

Born in Macedon in 356 BCE, Alexander had the philosopher Aristotle as his tutor by the age of 16, but it was in battle that he displayed his brilliance. Ascending to the throne in 336 BCE, he immediately claimed and reclaimed a series of opposing empires, spreading Greece across the Balkans and down through India. It is said he tended towards megalomania, desiring to rule the whole world – and nearly succeeding.

What he could not conquer was death. At the age of only 32 he developed a fever, rendering him dumb, and 11 days later he died. Some believe he was poisoned. His body was placed in a gold casket, which was then filled with honey. He was off, they said, to conquer the heavens.

HELLENIZATION

India. Egypt. Persia. Alexander's conquests were almost beyond belief. He began by taking Asia Minor, as his father had attempted, and ended with much of the rest of Asia in his thrall. He founded more than 20 cities, including the city of Alexandria in Egypt.

But it is not just territory gained by which we measure Alexander's success and influence. In expanding the empire, he exported Greek culture across Europe and Asia, making it the dominant set of values and traditions for hundreds of years.

One example: language. The Greek language became the *lingua franca* (the common language) of the entire region, even through the years of the Roman and Byzantine empires which followed the Greek empire. In fact, it was not until the fall of the Byzantines in the mid-fifteenth century that the Greek language began to be supplanted.

The spread of Greek language, culture and citizens initiated by Alexander became known as the Hellenization of civilization – from *Hellas*, meaning "Greece". This is why the period following the death of Alexander is known as the Hellenistic period. The Western world, for the next few hundred years, really was Greek.

HELLENISTIC GREECE

The death of Alexander saw a new type of kingship adopted by the Greeks. The main kingdom was subdivided among Alexander's generals. History teaches us this is always a recipe for disaster, but the Greeks didn't have as much history to call on as we do! Inevitably, the various kings and their descendants went to war against each other, and it was not until the mid-third century BCE, almost a century after his death, that the kingdoms of Alexander's successors were stabilized, and agreed their borders.

Alexander's conquests had delivered huge numbers of new city-states to Greece, and there was a lot of emigration from the centre to places such as Alexandria, now party to what was known as the Ptolemaic Kingdom, and Antioch, in the Seleucid Kingdom.

But also in the third century BCE, a new power in the north was beginning to flex its muscles. Across the Ionian Sea lay a boot-shaped country, with which Greece had occasionally skirmished. It was now growing in strength, having become a republic, named for its capital city.

Its name was Rome.

ROME TRIUMPHANT

There are various dates given for when the Greek Empire ended, but by the mid-second century BCE, Rome had absorbed most of eastern Greece in a series of wars. In 146 BCE the two empires engaged in what was known as the Achaean War.

The war saw a number of Roman victories, as the fighting closed in on the capital of the Achaean League, Corinth. Nearly 30,000 Romans marched on Corinth, which was defended by about half as many men. The battle took barely 48 hours, with the Greeks fleeing and their leader Diaeus committing suicide. The Romans then sacked the city, destroying it and many of its artworks, although some were also plundered. Greece was now under Roman rule.

An empire that had lasted around 1,500 years was over. But unlike some other empires, it was not to fall into obscurity. Some of those empires exist for us only in history books, but Ancient Greece exists all around us, in the way we live and the way we think. There are many aspects of our lifestyles that an Ancient Greek would recognize, and many things in their lifestyles would seem very familiar.

EVERYDAY LIFE

The story of any empire is the story of big battles, of lands conquered, rules made, systems of government put in place. It is the story of famous people who have left their stamp on human history.

It is also the story of day-to-day lives and loves, of people going about their business. What was it like to be an Ancient Greek? What was it like to live there, to learn there, and to earn there? Fortunately, this first properly recorded civilization has left us plenty to work with, so let's go back there and see exactly what was going on...

GOING BACK IN TIME

As we have seen, the Ancient Greeks not only lived, they thought about how they lived, and how they should live. Just as importantly for us, they also wrote down the details of their existence in ways unseen in earlier civilizations. We can't know every detail, but we do have a very clear picture of the daily life of individuals, societies and the state.

And given how much of Greek culture has filtered down to us, it doesn't take a giant leap of the imagination to put ourselves in their shoes – or sandals! We can recognize many of the activities they took part in, the institutions they attended, the families they raised and belonged to, even what they ate and drank.

So, let's pop back around 2,000 years to Greece in all its glory, where you might bump into the father of philosophy, Plato, the father of history, Herodotus, or the father of mathematics, Euclid. There are plays to be seen, musical performances to attend, political parties to join, gods to worship and worlds to conquer.

HOUSE AND HOME

Despite the dominance of cities in the history of Ancient Greece, the majority of the population lived in rural villages, in a subsistence economy. Houses were simple affairs, built out of mud bricks or wood, around a courtyard or garden. Windows were empty, but would be covered with a wooden shutter to keep out, or in, the heat.

Furniture was scarce – the main piece being a bed, stuffed with wool, feathers or dry grass. Richer families, and ones from urban areas, would decorate their homes with paintings or tiles. There were no bathrooms – people either attended public baths, or just used a bucket or a stream.

The only room that would seem odd to us is called an "andiron" – part of a Greek house that is reserved for men, used for entertaining male guests. With couches placed around the room, men could get together and discuss masculine things. Again, in poorer houses these did not exist – apart from the lack of space, there was probably a lot more work to get done!

The importance of the Greek home is reflected in the word *oikos*, a central concept in Greek living.

OIKOS

In its most basic form, *oikos* simply means a house that a family lives in. However, over time the word took on wider and deeper meanings – the family itself became the *oikos*, then the family group, including relatives, and later groupings that were not dependent on what we call genetics. Your *oikos* was where you came from, your community, your home.

Its importance as a concept can be seen in the number of words derived from oikos – many of our words starting in eco- have *oikos* as the root. For instance, the "economy" is the management (*nemein*) of the household. "Ecology" is the study of our home – *oikos* and -*ology*, which means, of course, that our home is the environment around us.

For the Greeks themselves, extending the meaning of *oikos* also reflected the way that they extended the meaning of what it was to belong. Places they colonized became part of Greece's *oikos* – they were not just subject states, but part of the Greek "family" and culture. This was a new type of empire.

It was also the building block of a new type of location – the *polis*.

THE POLIS

A Londoner, Parisian or New Yorker. Nowadays, it is common to refer to people as belonging to a particular city, by which we mean belonging to a particular tribe, and a particular set of values. It is an idea that originated with the Greeks, and it stressed things like freedom, equality and duty – the latter in the form of citizenship.

Although every city-state was different, one model came to dominate and in many ways define the polis. There was a central town, usually walled, and on the highest point was built an "acropolis" – literally the "summit" (*akron*) of the city. Here the main religious and municipal buildings were located. There was also a marketplace called the "agora". This was for commercial enterprises, but also to gather and carry out religious, political, social and philosophical discussions and debates (to this day "the marketplace of ideas" is a metaphor for philosophical debate).

As the *Encyclopaedia Britannica* puts it, "Ideally, the polis was a corporation of citizens who all participated in its government, religious cults, defence, and economic welfare and who obeyed its sacred and customary laws." This was the definition of citizenship.

There were of course limits to who could be a citizen, and any polis would contain a sizeable number of noncitizens. Women, for instance, could not be citizens; nor could foreigners or slaves. Male children had to attain citizenship, which required not just becoming older, but often declarations of loyalty.

In his masterwork, *The Republic,* the philosopher Plato has his teacher, Socrates – the mouthpiece of much of his work from around 375 BCE – attempt to define the ideal polis. There are, he argues, five main economic classes of any polis: merchants, sailors/shipowners, producers, retailers and wage earners. There are also four virtues of a polis: wisdom, courage, moderation and justice. The ideal polis would have equal shares of each of these.

To live in the polis in Ancient Greece was, therefore, to be part of a greater project. It was to live a life of duty – to do whatever one did well, and for the benefit of all. It was an idea that Greece would spend a long time exporting, along with the ideas that were being generated by this new experiment in living.

SOCRATES

There had been philosophy before Socrates, but as the Internet Encyclopaedia of Philosophy puts it, "Socrates is one of the few individuals whom one could say has so shaped the cultural and intellectual development of the world that, without him, history would be profoundly different." His method of question and answer, known now as the Socratic method, changed philosophy absolutely – for many, he is indeed the father of philosophy.

Famously, Socrates – born in 469 BCE, and a soldier in his early adulthood – never wrote anything down. Instead, he would accost citizens and interrogate them about their ideas and about truth. A school formed around him, and the Socratic dialogues they engaged in set out the terms for all future philosophy.

But for Socrates, it came at the cost of his own life, as asking too many questions was to make people uneasy. His methods annoyed the wrong people, and he was sentenced to death for the crime of impiety and "corrupting youth". Refusing offers to escape, or to be sent into exile, he drank hemlock and died in 399 BCE, aged 70. Two and a half thousand years later, his name lives on.

COUNTRY LIFE

Outside the polis, things were much more bucolic (from the Greek word *boukolos*, meaning "herdsman"). Then, as now, the climate of Greece was warm and dry, and most people were employed in fishing, trade or farming. In fact, around 80 per cent of Greeks were involved in farming and agriculture. And a lot of what they produced and ate is still produced and eaten today.

For a Greek farmer, the main vegetable crops were cabbages, onions, garlic, lentils, chickpeas and beans – although some Greeks avoided beans, believing that the souls of the dead might rest in them!

Olive trees were plentiful, producing fruit and oil, while there were extensive orchards of fig, almond, apple, and pear trees. Then, as now, dates were a standard part of the Greek diet.

But larger than all of these was the cultivation of grains and cereals, of wheat and barley. In fact, the goddess of agriculture, Demeter, was sometimes known as "she of the grain". The Greeks were one of the first civilizations to develop bread-making techniques and to make bread a key component of their diet – another idea they gave us.

MEAT AND FISH

While very little of their agriculture was centred around producing meat, the Ancient Greeks were not vegetarians. Goats and sheep were the most common livestock – easier to rear than cattle, and providing a plentiful supply of meat, wool and cheese.

They also kept chickens, while horses were seen as a luxury item only affordable by the very rich. Some animals, such as oxen, were used to help with working the fields, but this was rare – it was more down to the sweat of the farmer's brow (or in some cases, the sweat of the slave's brow).

In a place where there are many islands and lots of coast, fish were plentiful – squid, octopus, cuttlefish, prawns and crayfish were common, as were anchovies and sardines. Other fish, such as mullet, bass, swordfish and tuna were also devoured, often salted, as were eels.

Of course, with somewhere as large as the Greek Empire, there were many regional variations. But wherever in Greece you went, there was one staple that everyone could agree on: wine.

THE ELIXIR OF THE GODS

There is no getting away from it: the Ancient Greeks liked a tipple. The Mediterranean palate is made for wine, just as the Mediterranean soil is made for growing grapes. Mixed with a little water – to do otherwise was considered barbaric unless it was for ill health or to cure travel sickness or melancholy – wine was present at all social occasions, and unsocial ones!

The apotheosis – a Greek word derived from *apo* (from) and *theos* (the gods), and meaning the "highest point" – of wine drinking was at the spring festivals of Dionysus, the god of wine. For three days, participants celebrated the coming of the warmer weather by engaging in what can only be called drinking competitions – drain your cup the quickest, win the biggest prize!

What the Greeks themselves didn't drink, they exported. The importance of the wine trade can be seen in the many Greek coins that carry pictures of vines. They also exported knowledge, with new techniques in viniculture helping to establish wine growing in places like Spain and Portugal. They might have also introduced wine to southern France – where the idea certainly caught on!

HESIOD

Not all early Greek poetry was in the form of epics like those of Homer. In around 700 BCE, the poet Hesiod produced the poem "Works and Days". It is what we might call a farmer's almanac, with the poet advising his brother Perses on how to look after their land.

Much of the advice is moral, often to do with the virtues of hard work – apart from anything else, Hesiod notes, it keeps you from stealing, being jealous of others, and you won't shame yourself by begging.

There is a lot of practical advice about agriculture, too, from what to wear on your feet ("As for your feet, fasten onto them tight-fitting boots made from the hide of a slaughtered ox and make them snug with felt on the inside") to what sort of hat to wear and why ("On your head wear a shaped hat made of felt. This way, your ears will not get wet."). Farmers are advised to get to work before dawn to avoid the heat of the sun, and to get a dog ("do not begrudge him his food").

Whether Perses took the advice is not recorded!

TRADE

Of course, not all of the goods that farmers like Perses were producing were for the local market. Ancient Greece was one of the greatest trading nations the world has ever known, exporting olives, figs, cheese, honey and yes, wine, to countries throughout the world. It was also a huge exporter of pottery – examples have been found as far afield as the Atlantic coast of Africa.

In return, Greece imported textiles, glass, papyrus, wheat and slaves. This was largely done through private enterprise – the state had little influence, and things like tariffs and taxes barely existed. The state did, however, provide coins, another Greek invention. Originally made from electrum, an alloy of gold and silver, they were soon made of silver only.

As the empire spread, so did trade routes and the reach of Greek currency – from southern Italy and Sicily, to Egypt, Carthage, Ethiopia and the Arabian Peninsula. For commercial travel, sea was usually the preferred route – the placid waters around Greece made it the easiest way to go, while mountains prevented the building of proper roads. Whoever the "father of roads" was, he was likely Roman not Greek!

DEMOCRACY

The growth of the idea of the polis went hand in hand with another idea which was new and radical at the time: democracy. From the words *demos* (people) and *kratia* (power), "democracy" means "people power" – the right of citizens to determine how they are governed.

Most famously adopted by the polis of Athens, democracy is estimated to have existed in around half of the over one thousand Greek city-states that existed by the late fourth century BCE.

Before this, city-states tended to be run by *archons*, magistrates charged with keeping public order, who originally served ten-year terms though these were later reduced to one. They were chosen by fellow aristocrats or appointed by kings.

In the new democracies, each year, 500 citizens were chosen by lot to serve in government for a year. They were responsible for proposing new laws. For a new law to pass, all the citizens of the city gathered in the agora and voted. Today, this would be known as direct democracy, as opposed to representative democracy – it is a form of referendum, rather than the type of government generally convened in Western nations in the twenty-first century.

As we have seen, not everyone in the polis was regarded as a citizen. Women, children, foreigners and slaves were excluded from citizenship and therefore from serving in government and voting on laws. For example, it is estimated that the number of people qualified to vote in Athens was only around 30 per cent of the population.

Democracy had its critics, too, although many of these criticisms centred around undesirable outcomes of democratic laws, which were then ascribed to the system itself. A battle lost under democracy tended to be criticised as a battle lost *because* of democracy.

One of the most trenchant critics was the philosopher Plato, who feared that democracy would lead to irrational decisions, to only selfish people gaining power, and that the masses might be inclined to choose popular tyrants rather than wise men.

What do you think?

Of course, Plato's arguments might also have been coloured by an unfavourable outcome – it was a democratic vote that condemned his teacher Socrates to death. This would not have happened, argued Plato, under a wise ruler, and he had just the sort of person in mind...

PLATO

Philosopher A. N. Whitehead put it simply: "All of Western philosophy is but a footnote to Plato." It is to Plato that we owe our knowledge of Socrates – many of the books Plato wrote record the dialogues of the man who famously never wrote anything down. But that is just a part of his vast corpus. In Plato's writing, we find not only many of our deepest philosophical ideas, but works on the creation of the universe, on law and ethics, on politics and on poetry.

Born in Athens in 427 BCE to an aristocratic family, Plato was originally called Aristocles. He only acquired the name Plato later – it means "broad", and refers to his forehead. His obsession with philosophy started young – indeed, he was one of the youths Socrates was said to have corrupted. By the age of 40 he had established his own school named the "Academy", our source of the word.

In his greatest work, *The Republic*, he sets out his idea of the ideal state, and his idea of an ideal ruler: a philosopher!

He never got the job, and died in 348 BCE, but he does remain the king of all philosophers.

WOMEN

Ancient Greece didn't invent misogyny (*misos*, meaning "hatred"; *gunē*, meaning "woman"), but it may have perfected it...

Even the greatest fan of Ancient Greece would be hard pressed to see it as a society where being a woman was an advantage. In Athens, women were generally married off between the ages of 12 and 15, transitioning from living under their father's rule to living under their husband's rule. They were generally restricted to the house and were banned from owning private property. Ironically, poor women had more freedom than rich ones – if their husband couldn't afford as many slaves, his wife might be allowed to go out and do the shopping!

While all children of citizens were entitled to an education, girls were only trained to be good wives. What's more, the mentor of a young girl was legally free to engage in a sexual relationship with her. Once married, a woman's role was to run the household and stay faithful – neither was expected of her husband.

There were some exceptions, and some philosophers argued against this mistreatment of women. But this was no hotbed of feminism to say the least!

HIPPARCHIA OF MARONEIA

One woman did push back against the misogyny, Hipparchia of Maroneia.

She was born in 300 BCE in Maroneia in Thrace, to a well-to-do family that moved to Athens when she was young. Her early life was conventional, until she met a man.

And not just any man. Crates of Thebes was a Cynic philosopher. Cynics rejected all conventional desires for power, glory, social recognition, wealth, conformity and all possessions. Her family did not regard him as an ideal husband for their daughter, especially when he stripped naked in front of them to propose marriage! She accepted, even if they did not.

She too became a philosopher. They wore the same clothes as each other, and lived as equals, which was unheard of in those times. Nor did she occupy herself with weaving and organizing the household servants as was traditional. Instead, she engaged in philosophical disputes, as well as enacting her philosophy of subverting normal rules by bathing, speaking and even having sex in public spaces.

She remains an inspiration for feminist thinkers, who invoke her in challenging gender roles and overturning male oppression.

SPARTAN WOMEN

One exception to this patriarchal society – "patriarchal" being from the Greek, *patriarkhēs*, meaning "the rule of the father" – was in Sparta. It would be a stretch to say there was equality, but Spartan women could legally own and inherit property, and were usually better educated than their Athenian counterparts.

Education was still limited to household management, but there seems to have been a much higher rate of literacy among Spartan women. And, as well as reading and writing, women studied *mousike* – not just music, but also dance and poetry (our word "music" comes from this Greek word, meaning "art of the Muses"). They also participated in athletics.

As we have seen, the Spartans tended to be a warrior race, which meant the men were often off fighting battles. This in turn meant that the hearth and home were very much the female domain. According to sources of the time, they also showed dedication to battle – there was nothing worse for a Spartan woman than to have a cowardly son.

It is not quite feminism, but compared to much of Ancient Greece it was as close as they would get.

FERTILITY RITUALS

Children and childbirth were highly valued in Ancient Greece. For poorer, agrarian families, children were needed to help work, and then inherit, the land. For richer families, to be childless was to risk losing all property on death – no wonder there were a lot of rituals around childbearing!

Foremost of these rituals was the festival of Thesmophoria, which went on for three days at harvest time. Attended by wives only, it was a celebration of fertility – human, animal and agricultural.

Dedicated to the goddess Demeter and her daughter Persephone, rituals were carried out to bring on pregnancy. Pigs were slaughtered and offered up to the goddesses, along with cakes baked in the shape of snakes and phalluses. Free of the fetters of men, during the festival, the women were free to celebrate their own sexuality.

The purpose of the festival was ultimately serious – particularly for the women, for whom being childless was seen as a form of failure, which could have terrible consequences. Men were free to leave women who did not produce offspring, which would then mean they were banished from society, and fated to a life of poverty or prostitution.

CHILDHOOD

So, what was it like to be a child in Ancient Greece? It was to be in a position of some responsibility. Boys and girls grew up together until the age of seven, playing games together and residing in the woman's quarters (*gynaeceum*) of the household with their mother.

At seven, the boys would be sent to school, where they would be prepared for a life as good citizens, as warriors or in politics. Some were later trained to become philosophers or artists. At 15, education ended except for elites, who would attend a gymnasium for two years. On graduation, they cut their hair as a sacrifice to Apollo, and all boys were expected to do military service for two years.

For girls, of course, education was mostly about being good wives and householders, and took place at home. To learn to cook, sew and tend for their own future children was the highest achievement of girlhood.

Despite the focus on preparing for adult duties during childhood, there are many passages in Greek poetry and literature from Homer onwards that show huge affection for children – boys and girls!

RELIGION

As we have seen, Ancient Greece was a polytheistic society – there were many gods, related to different parts of everyone's lives. Daily religion was mostly about praising these gods and offering them sacrifices, such as bulls, sheep or poultry, in order to appease them and bring good luck. These sacrifices often happened at festivals at which a particular god was celebrated.

Although they were believed to be immortal, the gods were certainly not all-good or even all-powerful. They had very human characteristics, being prey to jealousy, anger, love and hate. They fought battles among themselves over the fates of those on Earth and those in the heavens. To be favoured or protected by a particular god allowed a human to thrive – but don't fall out of favour, or the consequences could be horrendous!

In Ancient Greece, there were no churches in the sense we are familiar with. Instead, the Greeks built huge numbers of temples, which tended to be dedicated to one particular deity. Some of these temples remain standing today, such as the Temple of Athena Parthenos in Athens, which is among the greatest works of architecture in the world.

ZEUS

Although there was no "supreme being" in the sense that we understand it, there was a hierarchy of the gods and at the top was their king, Zeus. He lorded over 12 major gods and goddesses who made their home on Mount Olympus. Zeus himself was the sky-god, sending thunder and lightning down at Earth, especially when he was angry. And Zeus got angry a lot.

Many of the Greek myths and beliefs are built around the clashes of the various gods and goddesses with each other, and Zeus was often front and centre. He was married to Hera, the goddess of marriage, women and family. He also indulged in numerous affairs with human women, stoking Hera's jealousy. His offspring from these affairs include Heracles (known to the Romans as Hercules), the Greeks' greatest mythical warrior.

Although humans were not thought to be the creations of Zeus, he was supposed to watch over Earth and our affairs with a father's eye. It was he who punished Prometheus for revealing the secret of fire. It is believed that to this day Prometheus remains tied to a cliff, with an eagle eating his liver, which regenerates every night. Never cross Zeus!

ORACLES

As well as gods and goddesses, the Greeks paid heed to oracles – priests and priestesses who could tell of the future. Oracles were thought to be portals through which the gods spoke directly to people. The gift of prophecy was passed from one priestess to another over the centuries.

The most famous of these priestesses was the Oracle of Delphi, based at the Temple of Apollo in central Greece. She was named Pythia, and is generally written of as a woman in her 50s who lived apart from her husband.

People – not just simple citizens, but kings and generals – travelled for many miles to consult the oracle. Before battles, she was consulted on tactics and outcomes, and many generals rode into war with either composure or foreboding based on her prophecies.

To citizens, she responded to questions about war, law, crime, family, duty, politics and personal issues. They say she was never wrong, although some of her statements did have an ambiguous nature. But if the questioner failed to understand the meaning it was their problem not hers!

CLOTHING

And what might one wear to visit the oracle? Pretty much the same as any other day. Ancient Greeks were known for the simplicity of their clothing, whatever their class. There were two typical garments: a tunic and a cloak.

Two types of tunic were common. One was the *peplos*, which was a large rectangle of heavy fabric, usually wool, folded over along the upper edge and reaching down to the waist, and fastened at the shoulders with a brooch. The other type was called a *chiton*, made of a much lighter material. It was a very long and wide rectangle of fabric sewn up at the sides, pinned or sewn at the shoulders, and usually girded around the waist. Both types of tunic were floor length for women, but could be knee length for men.

Most representations of Ancient Greek clothing show it as being white, but this is because much of our knowledge comes from marble sculptures. In fact, most clothing was coloured, using natural dyes from shellfish, insects or plants. Fun fact – the marble statues used to be coloured too: it's just that the paint has worn off!

ARMOUR

Of course, when there was war to be waged, the men would wear protective clothing of various types – and war, as we have seen, was often being waged.

Citizen-soldiers were called *hoplites*, and most of their protective clothing was geared towards one-on-one combat – Greek battles tended to be up close and personal, as Homer's poem *The Iliad* shows us.

The upper body was covered in a *linothorax*, which translates as a linen breastplate. This was many layers thick and stuffed with loose fibre to give it depth. Later, bronze breastplates were used, but their greater strength was offset by being much heavier, so not everyone wore one.

A helmet was also worn, and over time these became lighter, and did not impair the wearer's hearing and vision so severely. Many had horsehair crests for decoration, and to help identify military units. A shield, called an *aspis*, was also carried, and some of these had elaborate designs for higher military ranks.

Those on horseback generally wore lighter armour, would be bareheaded, and carried smaller shields. They would also be sleeveless, to free up the arms. It was no job for the fainthearted.

WAR

For the average Ancient Greek, there was bound to be a war or two during their lifetime, either against foreign aggressors or against other parts of the Greek empire. There was not really a professional army – instead all male citizens were called on to do their duty, although those over 60 were generally exempted. A *hoplite* would usually be called up from another profession, to which they would return after the war, if they survived.

Wars tended to be short, bloody and decisive. The two armies would march to the place of battle, attack each other head-on, and then declare a victor. Sometimes an individual champion of the battle was chosen – he might be of any rank, and his performance would be lauded by both sides.

Important to Greek warfare was the formation called the phalanx – a rectangular mass of *hoplites* tightly packed together that would advance slowly on the enemy, before rushing into the fray. With their shields held before them, the phalanx would make a group defence against the enemy. Alexander's armies deployed the phalanx often, but it eventually foundered against the Romans, who employed more flexible methods.

DEATH RITUALS

Whether you died in battle or in another way, death rituals were hugely important to the Greeks. It was generally believed that at the moment of death, the spirit of the body, called the *psyche* – a familiar word to us – would leave the body.

The body then underwent funeral rites, and to fail to do these was seen as an insult. In fact, so important was this that many Greek plays and poems explore the notion of disrespecting a dead man – from Hector being towed around Troy in Homer's *The Iliad*, to the heroine in Sophocles' *Antigone* being willing to die to make sure her brother is properly mourned.

During the funeral rites, the body was washed and anointed with oil, and friends and relatives would gather for a lamentation. Then there would be a funeral procession, usually just before dawn. Finally, the body would be interred and elaborate statues were often erected to mark the grave. Of course, for poorer people, a simple stone would do.

Accounts vary on what the Greeks believed happened to the soul after it left the body, but we do know one place you might end up: the Underworld.

THE UNDERWORLD

The Greeks believed in an afterlife, and from the time of Homer onwards there are myths about the Underworld, ruled over by Hades, the brother of Zeus. The deceased enter the Underworld and are carried by the ferryman, Charon, across the River Styx. There they might spend eternity in the Asphodel Meadows, about which we know little, or, if of high rank, in the Elysian Fields, a utopian paradise.

No mortal was allowed into the Underworld, although there have been exceptions, most notably Orpheus, the legendary musician and poet. On the death of his beloved wife Eurydice, Orpheus was allowed to descend to the Underworld to bring her back. There was only one condition: he must walk in front of her and not look back until both had reached the upper world.

He almost made it, but just as he was about to reach the outer gates of the Underworld, he suddenly feared Hades had deceived him, and that he would return to our world without his wife. He turned to check she was there, and she was cast back down to the depths.

Only when he too died, were they reunited.

PEACE

Life was not all working, fighting and dying, however. The Greeks enjoyed their leisure time, and in the warmth of the Greek summers this meant a lot of time outside, indulging in many of the pastimes still enjoyed in the area today, like swimming, drinking, eating and sunbathing.

In fact, the philosopher Aristotle argued that when it comes to living well, the quality of leisure matters more than work, as long as it is constructive. People tend to waste their leisure time, he argued, but it should be a time when we can most be and develop ourselves.

One way the Greeks did this is, as we have seen, through sports. Outside the Olympics, Greeks engaged in chariot races, running races, and the still familiar pentathlon, featuring five events including such things as discus, long jump, wrestling and javelin.

There were also festivals to attend, and these would often feature large banquets and singing and dancing deep into the night. It's no surprise that the Greeks were among the first people to come up with a hangover cure: cabbage, and what we call Brussels sprouts!

FLUSHED WITH SUCCESS

It goes without saying that, when looking at the everyday life of any civilization, there is one question that any thorough researcher must ask: where did they, ahem, relieve themselves? The Greeks were not shy about bodily functions, and as ever they showed a great deal of ingenuity and common sense when dealing with their waste products.

The first ever flushing toilet? Greek, of course, located at the Palace of Knossos, dating back to the seventh century BCE. Channels were built into the wall of the bathroom which made it possible to flush waste with water that was held in cisterns. A drain in the floor took the effluent out to the nearest river, the Kairatos.

Not everyone lived in a palace of course, and smaller houses had no way of fitting a whole bathroom unit. Public toilets were common, and relieving oneself in front of others was actually seen as a sign of nobility. One went to a long bench, sat beside others, and did one's business in a trough running under the bench. There was no toilet paper; small stones were used.

We may be better off now!

THE ARTS

It is in the arts that the Greeks excelled themselves, so much so that the forms of entertainment they invented changed the world. Before the Greeks we tend to regard art as only serving a decorative purpose, or perhaps a religious one.

No doubt, Greek art served these purposes, too, but as with so much of Greek culture, many works are also an exploration of what it means to be Greek, what it means to be making Greek art, and what it means to be human.

Epic poems like those of Homer were not simply composed to entertain, they were also meant to give practical advice on how to live, on what constitutes virtue, and how states and people should act in different situations. These poems endure because, for all the changes in the ways we live, the basics remain the same: we need food, shelter and love, as did they.

One artform in particular caused a revolution in art and in thought. And it started when a man called Thespis came out from behind a curtain.

ART AND
CULTURE

Ancient Greece was a place of big ideas. Huge intellectual advances were being made in all the arts and sciences – in fact, it is hard to think of another culture that has generated ideas so prolifically. And it is even harder to think of another culture from which ideas have resonated so far down the years and across the world. Art, science, philosophy, mathematics – no form of human thinking was left untouched.

So, buy a ticket, polish your shoes, and let's do what any Greek looking for fun would do – let's head to the theatre.

ALL THE WORLD'S A STAGE

In truth, we don't know if there was a curtain. Or a stage. Or even a man named Thespis. Our source is Aristotle, who tells us that, in the sixth century BCE, Thespis became the first man to perform a poem as another person – he was, Aristotle writes, the first actor, and his performance the first play.

By the time Aristotle was writing about Thespis, some 200 years later, theatre had become central to Greek life. Hundreds of people would attend performances of plays written by playwrights whose names have come down the centuries – Aeschylus, Sophocles, Euripides, Aristophanes and Menander.

From *Oedipus Rex* to *Agammemnon*, from *Medea* to *Antigone* and *Prometheus Bound*, their works have not only endured, but taken on new lives. Even now the plays are revived, or are used as the basis for new plays and films. In fact, there would not be plays or films without them. Theatre introduced a new way of exploring the world, in a new structure, and the basics remain vital to this day.

ARISTOTLE

If Plato was prolific, then there is no word that does justice to one of his pupils, Aristotle. We have around 1 million of his words, but scholars estimate that is as little as one fifth of his output. As much a polymath as a philosopher, there are very few areas of human thought and being that Aristotle didn't explore.

We know little about his life, just that he was born in 384 BCE, joined Plato's Academy at 17, and later, as the tutor of Alexander the Great, observed law and power close up. He was one of the first philosophers to study logic.

But it is his *Ethics* for which he is most famous: the exploration of right and wrong, and how to live "the good life", and what "the good life" means. Many of the ethical problems he set out around 335 BCE are still hotly debated in universities today, and in any place where two people are arguing about how to behave. His presence is also felt in many of our laws and systems of politics.

Who knows what is in the missing 4 million words he wrote?

THESPIS

According to all accounts, Thespis was a poet, and there was some form of public performance resembling theatre before he arrived. This was almost certainly part of Dionysia, a festival in ancient Athens in honour of the god Dionysus. Like modern festivals, attendances were huge and there were a large number of performances.

One sort of performance was called a chorus, which involved proclaiming poems and sometimes singing. It was the genius of Thespis to put on a show where he spoke a prologue, and then interacted with the chorus in dialogue. We don't know what it was he performed, but we do know that the year was around 534 BCE. It is unlikely that either he or his audience knew he had just shifted Western art and culture. That said, he did win a goat for his performance.

Thespis lives on in our word "thespian" for actor, while the character he played would have been the world's first "protagonist" – from the Greek *protos*, meaning "first in importance", and *agonistes*, meaning "competitor for a prize" or "actor". And, of course, his first opponent would have been his "antagonist" – adding *anti-* to *agonistes*.

DIONYSIA

Held in March of each year, the festival of Dionysia was a huge event on the Athenian calendar. It is likely that it was attended by both men and women, and visitors would come from all across the Greek empire. There was song and dance, processions, religious rituals and much drinking and feasting.

There were also poetry and music competitions, which were very competitive, followed by the sacrifice of bulls to Dionysus, and more drinking and feasting. Many attendees then took to the streets and performed their own processions, albeit slightly zigzag ones!

But it was the following three days that were most eagerly anticipated. This was the tragedy competition, in which the finest playwrights in Greece would compete against each other for prizes. Remember Thespis's goat? Well, tragedy comes from the Greek *tragos* (goat) and *aeidein* (song of). Tragedy is literally the song of the goat.

One winner we have a date for was Aeschylus, who took first prize in 484 BCE, although we don't know what for. Was first prize still a goat? If so, it was his first of several!

AESCHYLUS

Aeschylus is known as the father of tragedy. Sophocles may have been more popular, Euripides more innovative, and the later Aristophanes funnier, but it is to Aeschylus that we owe much of what we still recognize as theatrical form – the stage, the proscenium, the protagonist, the conflict and the resolution.

Only seven of his estimated 90 plays survive, but each is a keystone of our theatrical and literary history, with his trilogy *The Oresteia* being preeminent. Like most of his plays, it is based on a combination of history and legend, and explores themes of guilt, shame, vengeance and justice. And as with any good play, there is plenty of murder and some extremely rude jokes.

The Oresteia won first prize at the Dionysia festival in 458 BCE, which was essentially the Oscars of its time, although we don't have Aeschylus's speech thanking the academy. It was his fourth and last victory – he died two years later. But 27 years after his win, his son Euphorion triumphed in 431 BCE. One hopes he dedicated his victory to his dad!

GOAT SONGS

The time between Thespis's innovations and the first prizes awarded for tragedy was a mere 50 years, but in that time the art form had not only developed, it had become so popular that it was the biggest event at the biggest festival in the world.

Most tragedies dramatize events from Greek mythology – spectators would have known the stories already, but that was not the point. Tragedy introduced a new way to tell the old stories, with heightened dramatic tension, and with new, intense moral problems being raised and explored.

Initially, the plays would feature a maximum of two actors plus the chorus, which commented on the action. It was Sophocles, a younger contemporary of Aeschylus, who introduced a third actor, and who made the reactions of the chorus more complicated.

All the actors were male, including for the female parts. The plays were often performed as trilogies, running from sunrise to sunset. These were sometimes followed by a satyr play, which was essentially a tragedy with farcical elements and a focus on bodily functions – meant to raise the spirits after the depression that the tragedy may have brought on.

POETICS

It was not just depression that the tragedies were said to bring on. In his great book on the arts, *Poetics*, Aristotle theorized that tragedy could be explained by two things.

The first was *mimesis*. This means "imitation" – the actors imitate human affairs and bring them into focus. More importantly, tragedy causes *catharsis*, an Ancient Greek word still used in English today, and meaning "cleansing". By watching a tragedy, we are emotionally cleansed, which explains the burst of excitement we might feel at the conclusion of a work that has very dark content.

A good comparison is the horror genre. By rights, human beings should derive no pleasure from watching these films, and yet we can't look away, and there is a certain feeling of exhilaration at their conclusion. A negative emotion has been aroused, and when it leaves us we feel purified.

We have also had an "education" for our emotions. Where we might have intellectual responses to things like philosophical works, in tragedy it is our emotions that respond, and the way they respond can help teach us how to be moral.

REALISM

Once Aeschylus had laid down the rules of tragedy, and Sophocles had rebelled against them, other playwrights experimented with the new form – foremost among these was Euripides. His father was a shopkeeper, and when an oracle told his father that Euripides was destined to win prizes, he was immediately enrolled in an athletics school. He was not the last boy to find out he was more arty than sporty.

Slightly younger than Aeschylus and Sophocles, Euripides brought a new realism to Greek tragedy. Where his older contemporaries made characters into symbols of various virtues, Euripides brought new psychological depth to them, in ways we might recognize today. In short, his characters had feelings.

His other innovation was less subtle: the *deus ex machina*, literally meaning "god from the machine". Basically, when things got too complex, Euripides would have a god descend from the skies (on a pulley, hence "machine") and solve it all. Something of a cheat, although at the time, the sheer wonder of the mechanism was said to bring on a feeling of such astonishment in the audience that the moral effect of the drama was heightened. People love special effects.

YOU HAVE TO LAUGH

Tragedy was one of three forms of Greek theatre. The second was comedy, from the Greek word *kōmikós*, meaning "laughter-making". Greek comedy is generally divided into three phases – Old, Middle and New – and they more or less follow the same path as tragedy, gradually becoming more realistic.

Not valued as highly as tragedy – comedies then as now were seen as light relief – comedy still had its star writers.

First among them was Aristophanes, who was working at the same time as the tragedians, and who was not afraid to ridicule them, or anyone for that matter. Plato was furious that Aristophanes' play *The Clouds* mocked Socrates, and he blamed the playwright for helping get the philosopher condemned to death. Nor was Aristophanes afraid to make scatological (from the Greek *skor*, meaning "dung") jokes or use sexual innuendo. In short, his comedies were very broad.

By the time of later playwrights, such as Philemon and Menander, in the years after the death of Alexander the Great, comedy became more subtle, with recognizable stereotypes who would become the stock figures of comedy right up to the current day. If you have watched a sitcom, you have seen the characters from the "New Comedy"!

SATYR PLAYS

The third form of Greek theatre was the satyr play, which was performed after tragedies as a way of sending the audience home in a good mood after a gruelling day of moral entertainment. These were close to what we might call burlesque. A satyr is a male nature spirit with the ears and the tail of a horse, as well as a permanent, exaggerated erection.

As can be imagined, the plays concentrated on bodily functions, such as farting and body parts, like breasts, bottoms and the ever-present erections. There was a lot of wordplay, such as puns, and the plays were valued for their pure entertainment, not for any moral lessons or logical plots.

The only satyr play to survive is *Cyclops* by Euripides. The main theme is eating – characters gorge themselves on food and expel it with equal enthusiasm (from the Greek *en-theos*, "to be possessed by a god"). For much of the play the main characters are drunk, and no doubt as the closing act at the Dionysia, their audience may have been too!

MUSIC

The word "music" comes from the word "Muses" – the daughters of Zeus, the inspirational goddesses of literature, science and the arts. We talk of artists being inspired by the muse, and in Greek times that was taken literally.

Music was a major part of Greek life, interwoven with theatre, poetry, myth and ritual. Many instruments that are familiar to us now have their precursors in Greek instruments. To take one example, the lyre is the precursor of many of our string instruments (and its importance can be seen in the word "lyric", used for the words of a song, or a type of poetry).

We also owe to the Greeks our forms of musical theory and notation. It was the school of Pythagoras that first identified the mathematical basis of musical sounds, so that they could be written down (and therefore repeated, or given to others to perform). Our word "acoustic" comes from the Greek *akoustos*, meaning "audible".

We can't be absolutely sure what Ancient Greek music sounded like, although a few fragments survive, including a verse from the play *Orestes* by Euripides – the oldest "soundtrack" we have!

PYTHAGORAS

Anyone who has studied maths at high school will be familiar with Pythagoras. His theorem that in a right-angled triangle, the square of the hypotenuse is equal to the sum of the squares of the other two sides, is often the first piece of algebra taught. This was one of his achievements.

Born around 570 BCE, Pythagoras was the first man to call himself a philosopher, meaning "a lover of wisdom". To him we owe the knowledge that the Earth is spherical, that the morning and evening stars are both Venus, and the idea of the human soul. The school that developed around him became the model for most educational facilities, as well as religious foundations. He also gave the first philosophical arguments for vegetarianism.

But if all he had contributed was in the world of music, he would still be revered. He was the first to identify the relationship between music and numbers, discovering that tuning depended on ratios. Every time a musician tunes their instrument, they have Pythagoras to thank.

And that is even before we look at his contributions to astronomy, architecture, religion, teaching, numerology, mysticism, art...

THE PLASTIC ARTS: POTTERY

As we have seen, Greek pottery was highly valued throughout the world, and was one of Greece's greatest exports. From *c.*1000 to 400 BCE, Greece produced an astonishing variety of pots, vases, plates and bowls, sculpted from clay, the finest of which was Attic clay. The distinctive orange-red colour consistency of the clay meant that the vessels made from it were highly valued.

In part, such value was to do with functionality, but it was mostly due to their beauty – their classical shape and the way they were decorated. It is possible to argue that we know as much about Greek life and Greek myths from their pottery as we do from their literature.

The vessels were made by potters and then decorated by painters. It is generally believed that one potter would have a workshop in which a number of painters were employed. Some designs were simple, but over time they became more and more elaborate, without losing the simplicity of line so valued in Greek art and thought.

The move from geometric shapes to what are called "black figure" designs was a revolution in itself.

BLACK FIGURE POTTERY

First produced in Corinth in around the seventh century BCE, black figure painting came to dominate Greek pottery design for two centuries. It is the zenith of Greek pottery painting. Gods, goddesses, mortals and mythical beasts jostle for attention on vases, while wars are fought around the circumference of bowls.

Simple at first, these designs became more and more detailed, with the skilled hands of the painter using fine brushes to render hair, clothing and facial expressions. The individuals depicted show emotions in their faces and their gestures, and a narrative can be read in them.

It is not for nothing that the Romantic poet John Keats (1795–1821) was moved to write his poem "Ode on a Grecian Urn", celebrating "O Attic shape! Fair attitude! with brede / Of marble men and maidens overwrought". The poem ends with the famous couplet, "Beauty is truth, truth beauty – that is all / Ye know on earth, and all ye need to know."

Perhaps no objects since Greek pottery have come so close to this ideal.

THE PLASTIC ARTS: SCULPTURE

Ancient Greek sculpture is generally divided into three ages, like Greek history itself: the Archaic, the Classical and the Hellenistic.

Early Greek sculpture was in stone, imitating Egyptian styles. From the first, the human body was seen as the proper subject matter for sculpture, and in a culture where the gods had human form, this meant that mortals and immortals could be rendered in more or less the same way.

One distinctive (and fun) feature of the early style is what became known as the "archaic smile" – early Greek statues are shown grinning somewhat inanely. Debates continue as to what this means – some argue it is a sign that the model was still alive, while some argue that it was a marker of status, as aristocrats throughout Greece carried the nickname "Geleontes" or "smiling ones".

Or might it be something much simpler? Perhaps giving the statue a smile was a solution to the complex problem of making a curved mouth on the block-like head of Archaic sculpture? Perhaps the statue is smiling at how difficult it all is?

CLASSICAL SCULPTURE

During the Archaic period, statues tended to be of gods and mythical beings, but during the Classical period, forms became more realistic and more human, perhaps inspired by ideas of equality, democracy and the polis. There was also a dramatic increase in technical skill, assisted by the new use of marble. Some sculptors, such as Phidias, began to be well known, where the Archaic sculptors tended to be anonymous.

It was Phidias who oversaw the design and building of the Parthenon, including the hundreds of statues that adorn it. Statuary moved from being a private investment, to a public good. Then as now, statues were used to decorate buildings, either freestanding or as decoration. Some of the latter are incredibly intricate and detailed, showing new levels of skill.

Other statues, of war heroes and politicians, were placed to edify and inspire the population. These could be found in public squares, as were tributes to the dead. Families would have their loved ones cast, then placed in cemeteries or other meaningful places. Some of these sculptures remain the most beautiful artworks of antiquity.

STATUE OF ZEUS AT OLYMPIA

The greatest of Phidias's – and of the Ancient Greeks' – statues was the Statue of Zeus at Olympia, once one of the Seven Wonders of the Ancient World. Standing about 12.4 metres (41 feet) tall, it was made of gold and ivory, and featured Zeus sitting on a huge throne. The throne featured painted figures and other images and was decorated with gold, precious stones, ebony and ivory.

It had been commissioned by the custodians of the Olympic Games in 435 BCE, to sit in the newly built Parthenon as a display of Greek power. To some, seeing the statue was like seeing the god himself, and the sheer size of it made people imagine that if he stood, the roof of the Parthenon would be broken open. This was Greece at its greatest.

It stood, or rather sat, for almost 1,000 years. The Roman emperor Caligula once ordered it be beheaded, and soon after he died, the statue is said to have laughed out loud. But the Romans had the final laugh, as the statue was destroyed during a purging of what were regarded as pagan cults.

HELLENISTIC SCULPTURE

The final phase of Ancient Greek sculpture was the Hellenistic, after the death of Alexander. For some, this is regarded as a period of decline, and certainly the magnificence and splendour of the previous age are missing. There is more focus on domestic scenes, featuring women and children, even family pets.

There were still some great works created, such as the Winged Victory of Samothrace and the Venus de Milo. The Winged Victory is now exhibited in a prominent place in the Louvre in Paris. Missing its head and legs, and standing atop a marble ship's bow, it was discovered in 1863 and immediately recognised as a masterpiece.

But statuary was now becoming more of a trade, like pottery, with increasing standardization instead of inspiration guiding the production. As the power of Rome grew, and that of Greece declined, there were fewer victories to commemorate.

In fact, the development and decline of Greek sculpture provides a powerful way of assessing Greek culture, from the basic Archaic sculptures to the sophistication and magnificence of the Classical, through to the less magnificent Hellenistic. Their art was an expression of their world.

PAINTING

If we know less about Greek paintings than the other arts, it is simply because so few have survived. But we do know that, according to some of the greatest writers of the time, painting was the most common and respected form of art, especially as wall panels, which would have been the equivalent of our portraits. Unfortunately, most have been lost.

As we have seen, however, painting of pottery showed incredible levels of skill and sophistication and no doubt this was brought to panel painting as well. We do have Roman copies of some of the works, and they remain astonishing.

We also have examples of *ekphrasis* – a written account of an artwork. The word is a combination of *ek-* (meaning "out") and *phrásis* (meaning "speak"), so it is to "speak out". This was seen as one of the great literary skills, and has its origins in Homer, who described the sword of Achilles. Later Greek poets would develop the art, and some of their vivid descriptions only make us regret the loss of the original picture more.

THE GREEK POETS

Homer and Hesiod were Ancient Greece's two great epic poets, and their works still stand as some of the greatest works in literature. Their mode was known as epic, which as the name suggests, covers great spans of time, history and human emotions.

A second form of poetry also developed in the Classical period of Greek history: the lyric. Initially written to be accompanied by the lyre (hence the name), it expresses personal emotions or feelings, typically spoken in the first person. It remains the dominant form of poetry to this day, as well as being the basis for much of our music. Greek lyric poets were, in some sense, the singer-songwriters of their day.

Most famous were the Nine Lyric Poets, the most famous being Pindar, well known for his strange and idiosyncratic verses. Most of his poems are odes celebrating athletic achievement, but he uses this as the basis for an exploration of a huge range of human emotions.

Only one poet was held in higher esteem: a woman named Sappho.

SAPPHO

They called her "The Poetess", to be set alongside Homer, whom they called "The Poet". For the Ancient Greeks, she was the only one who could compare with the great bard, and even now Sappho is held to be one of the most brilliant poets in all history.

Alas, most of her work is lost, and what remains is in fragments – we have only 650 lines of the estimated 10,000 she wrote, and only one complete poem. This is not simply because of the long passage of time since she wrote, but also because much of her work was burned between the ninth and twelfth centuries CE, on the orders of the pope.

According to legend, Sappho was born on the Greek island of Lesbos in 630 BCE, and was exiled to Sicily in 600 BCE – we don't know why – dying there in 570 BCE. She was famous in her own time for the vividness of her work, and for the way it explored, and expanded, the range of human emotions.

Her work remains an inspiration. Occasionally, another fragment is found, and each one reveals a new level of brilliance.

THE PHILOSOPHERS

Although he himself admired poetry, the philosopher Plato decreed that in the ideal polis, all poets would be expelled. Why? Because, he argued, they are spreaders of misinformation.

The word "poetry" comes from the word *poiesis*, meaning "to create", and what the poets were creating was an imitation of life. Plato believed life itself to be an imitation of the perfect forms that lie outside the world. He believed that everything (from humans to alarm clocks) has a perfect form elsewhere – that all the triangles in the world are inferior copies of the perfect triangle that exists elsewhere. He argued that life is one of the forms, and that poetry is therefore an imitation of an imitation.

Plato was seeking *truth*. This became, and remains, the fundamental quest of philosophy: what is true, what is real, how are we to live in a way that is true to our nature, and so on. Ironically, Plato used an allegory to show what he meant (perhaps not realizing that he was using a poetic technique). It is known as the Allegory of the Cave.

THE ALLEGORY OF THE CAVE

Plato asks us to imagine a group of prisoners chained in a cave, unable to turn their heads. All they can see is the wall of the cave. Behind them is a fire, and between the fire and them is a group of puppeteers with puppets, whom the prisoners cannot see and do not know exist. The puppets throw their shadows on the wall that the prisoners are facing. The prisoners mistake the shadows on the wall for reality, unaware that the real objects are out of sight.

Plato argues that this is how we live our lives, mistaking the shadows on the wall for the truth. Philosophy is a way for us to break free of these chains, turn our heads, and see that we were in error. We can learn to see the truth.

The Allegory of the Cave has remained one of the defining metaphors in philosophy, and philosophy is a discipline that continues to search for the truth. What "truth" actually is, continues to be debated, but the quest goes on.

OTHER PHILOSOPHERS

While Socrates, Plato and Aristotle remain the best known of the philosophers, they were only part of a large intellectual movement occurring in Greece at the time. There was Epicurus (341–270 BCE) for whom the good life was one full of pleasure and without pain – his name lives on in the word "epicurean", meaning "someone who likes good food and drink".

There was also Thales (626–c.548 BCE), who believed that the whole world was made up of one substance in many different states – he believed the substance to be water. But he also set down one of the basic commands of philosophy: "Know thyself."

And there was Heraclitus, active around 500 BCE and best known for his doctrine that "change" is the basic property of the universe – everything is always in flux, nothing stays still. His most famous saying is that "No man ever steps in the same river twice, for it's not the same river and he's not the same man."

Each is an example of a new way of being in the world – not simply living, but thinking, analysing, and trying to make things better.

ATOMS

One final philosopher – and there were many, many more – has become more important in the twentieth and twenty-first centuries: Democritus (*c.460–c.370* BCE). His name means "chosen of the people". We don't know much about his life, except that he was known as "the laughing philosopher" because he believed strongly in the value of happiness.

But it is another of his beliefs that has come into sharp focus recently – he believed that the world was made up of much smaller particles, which he called "atoms". Some 2,500 years before a man called John Dalton came up with a modern theory of atoms, Democritus had already predicted them. In fact, the word "atom" is from the Greek *atomos*, which means "uncuttable".

Atoms, Democritus believed (and we now agree), are too small to be detected by the senses; they are infinite in number and come in infinitely many varieties. Everything we perceive – fire, water, chairs, humans, and so on – is made up of atoms.

Plato thought Democritus a fool and his theory insane, and advocated that his books be burned. To which we can only say: Democritus 1, Plato 0.

BODY

Philosophers, as a rule, tend to focus on our brains and our thoughts, but the human body was also becoming a new object for investigation in ways that had not been considered before. There had been medicine before the Ancient Greeks, but much of it depended on a great deal of superstition – the play of the gods. It was the Greeks who began to heal and treat the body in ways that are familiar to us.

Not that the efforts of the gods were completely ignored, but Greek medicine also acknowledged the effects of location, social class, diet, trauma, beliefs and mindset. Theories were tested in ways that are similar to those used in modern science and could be rejected if they failed. And the theories were based on the natural rather than the supernatural.

The first true physician is said to be the god Asclepius. Have you ever wondered about the strange serpent around a staff that is used to symbolize medicine to this day? That is the Rod of Asclepius. Legend has it that he performed the first ever operations, using opium as an anaesthetic, but it was a mortal who really developed the science...

HIPPOCRATES

It has changed many times over the centuries, to incorporate new practices, new inventions and new standards of morality, but the Hippocratic Oath's main demand – to help whoever needs it and "do no harm" – remains a fundamental ethical code in the medical profession. Many medical schools still require students to take a version of the Hippocratic Oath at graduation, some two-and-a-half thousand years after it was first written down.

Known as the "father of medicine", Hippocrates, born in 460 BCE, was the first person to regard medicine as a science, rather than something to be dealt with by magic or mysticism. To him we owe many of our medical notions and practices – the idea that diseases are natural rather than due to magic or the gods; that they are environmental, often to do with diet or lifestyle; that they are curable by the use of therapies including drugs; and that they followed particular patterns – his use of "prognosis" (to "know before") was a radical new idea, and is still basic to medicine.

It is said he lived to be over 100 – reward enough for his endeavours!

SENSE OF HUMOUR

Although it dates back to Egyptian times, the Theory of Humours was one of Hippocrates' greatest theories, and continued to be the main theory of medicine right up to the seventeenth century.

The theory held that there are four "humours" – roughly moods – in the body: blood, phlegm, yellow bile, and black bile. The ideal state is that all four are balanced. If one comes to dominate, or to dwindle, the body is thrown out of balance, and becomes ill. Take for instance, phlegm – a state of calmness, from which we get our word "phlegmatic". An excess or deficiency of this is a problem – too much phlegm induces apathy, too little, rage.

The Hippocratic method was to always achieve balance. An imbalance in phlegm can be cured with vegetables, breathing steam, salt water, drinking peppermint tea and so on.

This may seem an odd theory to us now, but many of what we call "complimentary medicines" emphasize a holistic approach to disease and bodily health. And what is balancing the humours if not that? Perhaps Hippocrates, that theorist of humours, will have the last laugh?

THE HEALING ARTS

The idea that the body is a "thing" that can be manipulated in positive ways led to huge advances in anatomy. Take Erasistratus – working in the third century BCE – who is credited with two astonishing advances in medicine. First, he put forward the idea that the heart is not the centre of all our sensations (as the poets would have it, and often still do!) but instead a simple pump. One passage in his writings almost predicts the circulation of the blood, some 2,000 years before it was discovered to be the case.

Even more remarkably, he identified that the brain was operating through a system of nerves, down which travelled thought. He was not entirely sure how these thoughts in our head equate to impulses in our brain but then, neither are we.

He also hypothesized that what happens in the brain plays out in the body – particularly in the case of love. This was one ailment, he decided, that was incurable.

AGNODICE

Agnodice has been an inspiration for over 2,000 years. In her time, as at many times in history, women were banned from practising medicine. In addition, the practice of midwifery was regarded with great suspicion. But Agnodice was having none of it. Medicine was her passion, and she would follow it, whatever the cost.

The first references to her appear in the work of the Roman writer, Hyginus, who tells of her living in Athens in the fourth century BCE. In order to study medicine, she disguised herself as a man, cutting her hair short and wearing men's clothing. She helped women during childbirth, revealing in privacy that she was a woman to those who were intimidated by male doctors.

Legend has it that other doctors, losing clients to her, accused her of having affairs with the women she tended, so she was forced to reveal that she was a woman. She was arrested, put on trial and, according to Hyginus, won the case, and the medical profession then opened its doors to women practitioners.

WEIRD SCIENCE

As we have seen with medicine, the great advance in Greek scientific thought was what we now call the scientific method – a process based on the belief that things operate rationally, and you can perform experiments which may succeed or fail. You can then learn from these, and perform other experiments.

"Thinking" remained the most popular method – Aristotle argued that men had more teeth than women without bothering to count the teeth of his wife – but gradually the empirical method (from the Greek *empeirikós*, meaning "based on observation") became dominant. This was particularly true in the Hellenistic era when contact with other cultures, and their methods, was at its height.

Some scientists were way ahead of their time. We know that the idea that the Sun, not the Earth, was the centre of the universe was first put forward by Copernicus in the sixteenth century – except it wasn't! Back in around 280 BCE, Aristarchus of Samos had exactly the same idea. He even argued that the Sun is a star – and that the stars are other suns, very far away!

If he'd had a telescope to prove things, 2,000 years of astrology would have been very different...

TECHNOLOGY

We live, it is said, in the "technological age", but what is technology? It comes from a hugely important Greek word *techne*, meaning "a craft, skill or method of production", and for Aristotle, for instance, it was different from *episteme*, meaning "knowledge". We think, but we also make.

And what the Greeks made is astonishing.

Engineering was not unheard of before the Ancient Greeks – you don't build the pyramids unless you know how to make stuff – but the Greeks made huge advances in what we now would call basic engineering techniques and methods. Screws, gears, the use of steam for power, mills and casting – these are all solutions to problems that the Greeks have gifted us.

One example: the crane. If only the Egyptians had one of these when building those pyramids! Unfortunately for them, it was not until around 515 BCE that the winch and pulley system, which is basic to cranes, was invented. As we shall see, the Greeks were masters of large architecture, and the crane enabled them to build on a massive scale with smaller manpower.

The era of ramps was over!

Of course, not every Greek invention deserves to be celebrated. Did you know they also invented the alarm clock? Plato was said to own one, but the true inventor, Ctesibius, seems to have lived a couple of hundred years later.

Ctesibius mostly worked in pneumatics, inventing not only various pumps but the precursor of the pipe organ, and his greatest and most annoying invention was the alarm clock.

We don't know exactly how it worked, but it seems that you could preset it to make pebbles drop on a gong, or a series of air trumpets sound, at a particular time. Even then, the Greeks seemed to know this was not necessarily a good thing – his clock was known as a *clepsydra*, which means "water thief".

But Ctesibius would have had to get up pretty early to beat another man, generally regarded as the greatest of all Ancient Greek scientists...

ARCHIMEDES

"Give me a lever long enough and I will move the world." So said Archimedes, the greatest mathematician of Ancient Greece and one of the greatest of all time.

Born in Syracuse, Sicily, in 287 BCE, Archimedes was the son of an astronomer, and went into the family business. The list of his achievements would fill this book, but for starters, he anticipated modern calculus, measured the area of a circle and the surface area of spheres, approximated π, and made huge advances in optics and astronomy.

His most famous practical invention was the Archimedes Screw, which lifts water by rotating, and is still used today in water treatment plants and anywhere water needs to flow upwards.

He also invented various "war machines" for the army of Syracuse, used when the Romans sieged the city, including powerful catapults, and a "death ray" which focused the sun on ships, setting them on fire. These machines may have helped Syracuse, but not their inventor – he died during the siege in 212 BCE, killed by a Roman soldier.

CARTOGRAPHY

Nowadays, maps fit on our mobile phones – they are usually associated with apps, and we take it for granted that when we walk or drive from place to place, they will show us where to go, and offer us images of the terrain.

But the world of the Ancient Greeks was less certain, and as it expanded, the terrain grew less and less familiar. How could one set these new domains down on paper?

It is to the Greek philosopher Anaximander (*c.*610–*c.*546 BCE) that we owe the first attempts to chart the world that the Greeks were coming to know. His map of the world is very basic, but the idea behind it was radical: the world beyond our own location is a constant and can be sought out. This could be for trade, but also for the pleasures of encountering new ways of life. Greek thinking was never insular – it was about journeying to other places, and other ways of existing.

And if you are going to travel the world in a boat, you may need to avoid the rocks, using another Greek invention...

TO THE LIGHTHOUSE

According to Homer, it was Palamidis of Nafplio who invented the first lighthouse, and that is all we know of its creator. But it was around 305 BCE that one of the greatest constructions in Greek history took place.

The Lighthouse of Alexandria, like the Statue of Zeus at Olympia, was one of the Seven Wonders of the Ancient World. It stood for around a thousand years, before a series of earthquakes brought it down, and since 1916 archaeologists have been reclaiming sections of it from the ocean floor – around 3,300 so far!

Alexandria had been founded by Alexander the Great, but it was after his death that the lighthouse was commissioned. It stood around 118 metres (387 feet) high, for many years, being one of the tallest buildings in the world.

Built of sandstone and limestone, it was said to be so awe inspiring it barely needed a light to change the course of ships. But it did have a light – during the day a huge mirror would reflect the sunlight, at night a fire was lit.

ARCHITECTURE

The Lighthouse at Alexandria was magnificent – but in terms of architecture, magnificence was what the Greeks did. Throughout their history, the Ancient Greeks not only created some of the greatest buildings in human history, they invented styles and techniques that continue to inform our current thinking about architecture.

If there is one type of building that defines Ancient Greece, it is the temple. Often standing on a raised plateau above the polis, these buildings were meant to inspire awe – and they did, and still do.

Perhaps the greatest of all their temples is the Parthenon in Athens. Dedicated to the goddess Athena, it was built in the fifth century BCE to celebrate victory over the Persians. It still stands, and thousands of tourists visit it and remain awestruck. It is a masterpiece of its type and, as with so much of Greek thought and life, the key is a sense of proportion. The Greeks also believed in rules when it came it architecture – there was a standardization, but these rules allowed creativity to flourish.

The Greeks believed there was such a thing as perfection, and the Parthenon is a monument to this idea.

COLUMNS

The idea of standardization is most dramatically seen in the three styles of columns embraced by the Greeks: the Doric, the Ionic and the Corinthian.

The Doric emerged in the seventh century BCE, and was used for the Parthenon. Typically placed close together with concave curves sculpted into the uprights, they are the simplest of the columns, and remain popular.

But soon after, a new style emerged: the Ionic. These are more decorative, characterized mainly by their scroll-like ornaments. They also have a large base, and some elaborate designs imported from foreign buildings.

This becomes more evident in Corinthian columns. Things are even more elaborate, with ornate capitals and stylized acanthus leaves. It is believed the style was invented in the fifth century BCE by Callimachus, who was inspired by the sight of acanthus leaves left on the grave of a young girl.

Whichever style was adopted, Greek architecture represented a huge leap forward in technique, method and art. Again, Ancient Greece pointed the way forward.

A LASTING
LEGACY

What continues to astonish about Greek
culture is that much of it has seeped
into our own. If we look around us, we
see the achievements of mathematics,
geography, architecture and art; if we
look inside, we see the achievements
of philosophy and psychology.

These are strong foundations on which
we build, as did the Romans, and later
Christian and Islamic nations, as well as
secular ones, who took the lessons of the
Greeks to nourish their own traditions.
No doubt, in 2,000 more years, their
achievements will still be generating culture.

THE MOST INFLUENTIAL CULTURE

Throughout history, empires, kingdoms and nations have risen and fallen, some barely known to us, some, like Rome, carrying an outsize influence. But perhaps no earlier culture has left such an imprint on our own as the Ancient Greeks. Their world is fascinating in itself, but it endures so powerfully because it remains all around us.

From our political systems, our laws and ethics, our ways of building communities, the tools we use and the thoughts we think – we only need to peel back a few layers to find the influence of the Greeks on Western culture.

There is no doubt that something shifted in the way the Western world thought, and the shift happened in Greece during this era. Other cultures had analysed themselves before the Greeks, but it is to the Greeks we owe so many of our forms of self-analysis, and the art and intellectual culture that goes along with it. There is plenty of proof of this all around us, as we have seen. But, as should have become clear, it is also there in one of our most intimate possessions: language.

WORDS, WORDS, WORDS

Human beings speak and think in words. The way we divide the world by assigning labels to things, tells us who we are and what we care about, as well as both opening the ways we can understand something, and forming the limits of what we can think. Legend has it that the Inuit have 50 words for snow, because they need to define different types so precisely. Language is a tool for getting us close to the world around us.

And as we have seen, so many of our ways of thinking are given to us by the Greeks, and by Greek words. Take "philosophy", meaning "the love of wisdom" (*philo* is "love", *sophos* is "wisdom"). Prior to the Greeks, it may well have been that some parts of what we would call philosophical thinking had been done, but the Greeks recognized this thinking as a unique aspect of being human, and gave it a word, from which a whole discipline flourished. Once something is named, it takes on a life of its own. Thinking about thinking (and loving it) became a thing.

It is estimated that around 150,000 of our words have an Ancient Greek origin. These words are everywhere. If you use a word starting with ph-, it is almost certainly Greek – philosophy, physical, photo, phrase, philanthropy (which is the "love", *philo*, of "humans", *anthropos* – you can see where "anthropology" comes from, too).

A word like *psyche*, meaning "soul, mind or spirit", is there in psychology, psychic and psychopath, while *cathedra*, meaning "seat", is in fact the root of our own word "chair", but also "cathedral", which means "the place with the bishop's throne".

Acrobat. Butter. Dinosaur. Panic. Europe. Each of these words has a Greek origin. Do you live in a metropolis – as you know, *polis* is a city, but what does *metro* mean? It means "mother" – a metropolis is a mother-city. By breaking a word down, we can see how it came to be used.

Ancient Greek is one of the building blocks of our language, and you'd be an idiot not to understand this – *idiōtēs*, "a private person, individual". In other words, a non-citizen.

PHRASES, PHRASES, PHRASES

It is not just individual words that come to us from the Greek – there are a large number of common expressions we use that stem from Greek mythology and literature.

An Achilles heel is a vulnerable point, and it comes from the myth that Achilles, born a mortal, was given immortality by being dipped in ambrosia by his mother, Thetis – but the spot where she held him, on the heel, remained mortal. He died after being shot there by an arrow.

Ever opened a Pandora's box, shown the Midas touch, or been caught between a rock and a hard place? Then you have borrowed from the Greeks. Hopefully, in the latter case, you will eventually rise from the ashes – again Greek.

And if you have ever accused someone of crying crocodile tears – that is, not being genuine in their sadness – you have again pulled from Greek origin, based on their idea that crocodiles wept as they ate people. In fact, they do lubricate their eyes via their tear ducts, but only because they dry out.

AESOP

It is not just from myths that we draw some of our wisdom and sayings. Have you ever heard the story about a tortoise who won a race against a hare? Or a goose that laid a golden egg? Or a wolf that donned sheep's clothing? Then you have heard some of the fables of Aesop.

We know little about his life, but according to the Greeks he lived in the seventh century BCE, and legend has it that he was a slave who was, according to one account, "snub-nosed, swarthy, dwarfish, bandy-legged, short-armed, squint-eyed, liver-lipped – a portentous monstrosity".

One day he found himself in the company of the Seven Sages of Greece – seven men renowned for their wisdom. He told them stories, each of which, for all its simplicity, contained a moral at the end. The tortoise teaches us that slow and steady wins the race; the goose that too much greed can cost us everything; evildoers end up harmed by their own deceit. Hugely impressed, the sages gathered his stories, and the moral fable was born.

NOT BEING AN IDIOT

The fact that someone who is a private individual, not a citizen, was called an idiot in Greece gives us an insight into how important citizenship was to Greek thought, and it has remained a huge part of our own view of the world. To be a citizen of a nation is to be given certain rights, and be expected to carry out certain obligations.

The law, much of which also has its origins in Greek thinking, is there on the one hand to protect us, but also to set out what we can and cannot do, to tell us what is expected of us in return for belonging. Those who do not conform to the laws can be denied their rights as citizens.

And those who come to a nation can be asked to perform a citizenship test, pledging their allegiance to their new country, but also being offered its protection. This is a very Greek notion of inclusion – in Ancient Greece, conquered peoples were often made to swear allegiance to Greece.

The fact that women and slaves could not is, therefore, hugely significant...

DEMOCRACY

It meant, for a start, that woman and slaves could not participate in one of the greatest of Greek inventions: democracy. Winston Churchill said, "democracy is the worst form of government – except for all the others that have been tried", and it remains the cornerstone of Western civilization, almost defining it.

Of course, the original Greek democracy was partial – not just anyone could vote – but it still marks a radical departure from the idea of kings and emperors that predates it. Citizens were seen to have responsibilities, but also intelligence – the state could be entrusted to their care. This was part of a great experiment in collective endeavour.

Democracy at its best remains exactly this. Over its long history, it has obviously had its triumphs and disasters (women, for instance, were still denied the vote in virtually every democracy until the twentieth century!), but for the majority of the Western world, and many other nations, it defines government – by the people and for the people.

ASPASIA

She is as much a legend as a real person. Rumoured to be the lover of the statesman Pericles with whom she was rumoured to have a son, rumoured to be a courtesan, rumoured to have been tried for impiety, and rumoured to be a comic poet and/or a philosopher, she seems to be something of a mystery. Some even claim she never existed.

Aspasia is first mentioned in comic plays, where she is a figure of fun. The idea is established that she was a brothel keeper, and her sexuality is commented upon in a derogatory way. But soon after, she is mentioned, by Plato and Xenophon, in philosophical dialogues, where she is portrayed as an educated, skilled rhetorician, as well as a source of advice about marriage. Some even believed that Socrates regarded her as an influence on his thinking.

In our own time, she has been held up as a feminist icon – a strong woman who got her way. And she had a new life when the best-selling action game *Assassin's Creed Odyssey* made her the heroine. The legend continues!

THE RULE OF LAW

As we know, with great power comes great responsibility. In order to be citizens, and, therefore, in order to be allowed to vote, we must abide by the laws of the nation to which we belong, and it is to the Ancient Greeks that we owe a huge part of our legal systems.

In fact, it might be said that one Greek law is fundamental to the majority of legal systems in the world. This is known as "the rule of law" and comes to us from Aristotle's book, *Politics*, which states that all people and organizations within a country, state or community are held accountable to the same set of laws. There is no favouritism – a rich man is treated the same in law as a poor one, and a poor one is treated the same as the rich.

Sometimes this rule has been contested, or questions have been raised as to whether it is being applied. Some argue that favouritism does exist in law – after all, if you are rich you can afford better lawyers. But the mere fact that we see this as wrong is down to Greek thinking.

DRACONIAN LAWS

Why did the Greeks adopt democracy and the rule of law? Aside from philosophical reasons, many argue that it was a direct reaction to the rule of a man called Draco, who in the seventh century BCE laid down the first ever laws in Athens, by writing its constitution. This replaced the oral laws of the time, which were often based on blood feuds.

The laws were particularly harsh. For example, a debtor whose status was lower than that of the person to whom they owed money was forced into slavery. Stealing led to the death penalty with no exceptions, not even based on the value of what was stolen – famously a man was killed for stealing a cabbage.

The influence of Draco's laws can be seen in terminology we use almost 3,000 years later. Laws that are regarded as overly harsh or unforgiving are still described as "draconian". But there are a couple of Draco's ideas that we retain. He made, for instance, a distinction between intentional and unintentional murder, which we call manslaughter. The first led to the death penalty, the second to exile.

Better accidentally kill a man than steal his cabbage!

LEGAL SYSTEMS

While there was no jury system in the way that we are used to, late fourth century BCE Athens was getting close to this – Greek law established many of the norms we adhere to today.

The accused had the right to a trial, and the right to defend themselves or have someone else defend them. Although "presumption of innocence" wasn't codified until the Romans adopted it, the accused were generally protected by this principle, which holds that it is up to the accuser to prove the crime. This was done by presenting evidence, and then by carrying out a rational investigation and discussion on the guilt or innocence of the party involved. Punishment, too, was codified – certain offences led to certain sentences, and it was up to the lawgivers to apply these without fear or favour.

Of course, as with our current system, these laws and the punishment for breaching them could change and adapt over time. The "people" decided the laws, and had them reflect the society they wished to live in. The key word here was "justice", as it remains to this day.

OTHER LAWS

Not all law is about crime and punishment, and the Ancient Greeks helped establish many of the less spectacular aspects of our legal systems – things like family inheritance, and laws around business and trade. As the empire grew, became more complicated, and indeed richer, more and more guardrails and conventions were needed to make the system run.

One example that remains in place is the idea of corporate governance – a business should have an independent board. These, when able, should be selected randomly – that is, the members of the board don't have another stake in the business. They are also expected (in fact, ordered) to act collectively rather than autocratically (*autos* meaning "self", *kratos* meaning "power"). Here again we see the idea of democracy.

While the idea of tax was not generally applied, in times of war it could be levied on citizens, but the amount was dependent on wealth. This makes it one of the world's first progressive tax systems, one that has also been retained in all Western democracies.

BUILDING THE WORLD

As we have seen, many of both the practical and theoretical concepts of engineering come to us from the Greeks. Much of the mathematics that underpins everything from our architecture to our space travel has its origin in Greek thinking.

In architecture, we are still affected stylistically – the idea of columns, be they Doric, Ionic or Corinthian, remains part of our mode of design, while ideas about symmetry and proportion continue to inform our thoughts on what a building should be. It is no surprise that, in the nineteenth century, when the West was growing rich, the neoclassical style dominated – we are still surrounded by buildings from this era, denoting wealth and power.

More than this, the very idea of urban planning comes from the Greeks. The way they set out the polis, and what they built there – from religious buildings to governmental ones, from parks and gardens to traffic systems – remains central to our own ways of creating cities and villages.

HOW BUILDINGS STAND UP

And it is not just for architectural design that we owe the Greeks thanks; it is also in the engineering. Apart from cranes, which grew in loading capacity throughout the history of the Greek empire, allowing more and more massive buildings to be built, the Greeks invented many of the tools and clamps that we now take for granted.

They also invented the roof truss – that triangular object that gives us our sloping roofs. In the list of Greek achievements this may seem low down, but consider the ways in which it has affected our environment, not to mention our plumbing systems, as standing water is taken away down the slope of the roof and into gutters.

Trusses also enable buildings to increase dramatically in size – one of the main difficulties architects face is that walls naturally want to lean outwards, and the further apart from each other they are, the more they want to lean. Trusses are a simple and effective way to hold them in place, without causing much strain.

ALL IN THE NUMBERS

Underlying all of this, of course, is mathematics. We have already seen the way that Pythagoras gave us many of our theories, indeed it is to the Greeks that we owe trigonometry, the branch of mathematics concerned with relationships between angles and side lengths of triangles. This has been hugely important not just in architecture, but astronomy, surveying, optics and acoustics.

It is also vital in navigation. The Greeks were ocean-going people, for obvious reasons, and made huge advances in the way ships were built, and how they made their way around. The ability to locate latitudes and longitudes of sailing vessels, plot courses and calculate distances during navigation grew exponentially in Greek times, helping make Greece a naval and trade powerhouse. We still use their discoveries, even in the most modern of geolocators.

But perhaps the greatest of all mathematicians in Ancient Greece was a man whose field was geometry, and his principles underlie much of our mathematical system to this day. His name was Euclid.

EUCLID

Euclid is known, inevitably, as "the father of mathematics". He lived around 300 BCE, and we know very little about him. What we do know is his most famous work, *Elements*, which established the foundations of geometry that still largely dominate the field to this day.

In *Elements*, Euclid sets out what are the building blocks of geometry, and indeed, mathematics – points, lines and planes. By combining these we can make all the shapes and figures needed for maths. His genius was to realize that mathematics could be built up from a few simple rules – even the most complex objects are, in the end, variations of the simplest.

For the first time, mathematics was organized systematically and logically. Triangles, circles and squares formed the basis of everything – but by understanding them we can understand everything, perhaps even the entire universe.

He called the rules of mathematics "axioms", which comes from the Greek *axios*, meaning "worthy". This is some understatement – his rules have remained worthy for 2,500 years!

PHILOSOPHY OVER TIME

We have already seen how the Greeks not only invented philosophy, but laid down many of the ideas and rules that continue to govern it. And it is not just our own time that has been affected – the influence of Greek thought on Medieval thinking (and, therefore, by transmission, our thinking, too) was vast.

During the Medieval period, a huge number of Ancient Greek texts (forgotten until then) were found and translated. Philosophers such as Thomas Aquinas (c.1225–1274) attempted to reconcile Aristotle in particular, with Christianity. This was not always easy – Aristotle did not believe in a creator God, and believed the world to be timeless. But Aquinas did borrow the idea that God could only be known by analogies (He is *like* x), and that we know the world through our senses, not innately.

These concepts would have profound effects on the way the Church was organized, and also provide the seed of the Reformation – the difference between the Catholic and Protestant Churches can be found in some of this thinking.

HAVE YOU HEARD THE ONE ABOUT...?

"Television? The word is half Latin and half Greek. No good can come of it." So said the editor of the *Guardian* newspaper, C. P. Scott, back in 1926 when it was just being invented. He was right about the word – *tele* is Greek for "far off" and *visio* is Latin for "sight" – but debates continue about whether he was right in his analysis.

One cannot of course claim that the Greeks invented television, but insofar as most shows are based on the techniques of theatre, it is certain that there would be no TV without them. In fact, as we have seen, the distance between the comedies of Ancient Greece and the contemporary sitcom is not huge. The themes of Greek comedy, the use of stock characters and the love of bodily functions, remain to this day.

In fact, one of the oldest recorded jokes comes from Greece and would not be out of place in a sitcom today. A man visits a barber who asks him how he wants his hair cut. The man replies, "In silence."

STAGE CRAFT

Theatre was a revolution in the arts. Without the Ancient Greeks, there would have been no William Shakespeare for instance, a fact the playwright seemed aware of – his works abound with references to Greek mythology. One such example is Theseus and Hippolyta in *A Midsummer Night's Dream*. This play is set in Greece, to a large extent in Athens, and is full of nods to his precursors. Meanwhile, in the play *Troilus and Cressida*, Shakespeare reincarnates figures from Ancient Greek mythology such as Agamemnon, and his brother Menelaus. We are not sure how he accessed the earlier plays as very little was translated, but these myths are so embedded in Western culture, they may have simply been in the ether (from the Greek *aithein*, meaning to "burn" or "shine").

As we know, thespian, chorus, protagonist and catharsis are from the Greek, but so are episode, hypocrite, prologue, proscenium (where the action takes place) and monologue. We even get the word and the concept of the orchestra – from the Greek word meaning "a place where a chorus comes to dance".

PAGING DR FREUD

It is not just our literary arts that the Greeks have influenced. Take the case of psychoanalysis, that branch of psychology inaugurated by Sigmund Freud (1856–1939). One of Freud's key ideas was that of the Oedipus Complex.

In the play *Oedipus Rex* by Sophocles, Oedipus, fulfilling a curse, unknowingly kills his own father and marries his mother. When he realizes what he has done, he plucks out his own eyes, and goes into exile.

Freud was interested in why the play continues to resonate after all this time. He believed it was because in some sense we suffer the same curse as Oedipus – for those of us born male in a traditional family, our first sexual attraction is to our mother and we harbour murderous wishes against our father. He believed that these urges are primordial and unconscious, and our conscious mind represses them, and that part of the job of psychoanalysis is to uncover these urges.

Freud did not put forward a female equivalent, but his follower Carl Jung proposed the Electra Complex, again drawing on Sophocles, in which a girl is attracted to her father and harbours hostility to her mother.

AROUND THE WORLD

In this book we have concentrated on the Western world, but the influence of Ancient Greeks on other cultures has also been immense. Many books of Greek philosophy were translated into Syriac, Arabic and Persian in the Middle Ages, long before they arrived in English or other European languages.

This time, around the ninth and tenth centuries CE, was also notable for being the Golden Age in Islamic mathematics. To take one example, the mathematician, astronomer and geographer, Al-Khwarizmi (c.780–c.850), whose name gives us the word "algorithm", was steeped in the works of Euclid, and he also advanced our understanding of trigonometry.

And, of course, Greek art and architecture has always been in dialogue with the East – we need only remember that at its height the Greek Empire encompassed much of the world. The architecture of Byzantium is Greek in origin.

The Greeks also gave Byzantium the secret of Greek Fire, an incendiary weapon that stayed lit on water, and which won the Byzantines a fearsome reputation in naval battles.

THE UNIVERSE AND BEYOND

This brief survey barely does justice to the influence of the Greeks on our lives. Now that you have seen how wide the field of achievements is, you will no doubt find more. Once you start spotting how Greek words sound in our language, you will keep hearing them, which will no doubt lead you on to other discoveries.

In fact, it is doubtful that any other culture has had such a profound effect on Western culture. Pick up any newspaper, or read one online, and story after story will be about politics or law – how nations and people negotiate with each other and set limits on what is and is not allowed. The Greeks could not have imagined the globalized world we live in, but we could not understand it without their contribution, nor could we have reached distant lands without their technology and innovations.

And not just on Earth – the Greeks first calculated the distance to the moon. Could they have imagined one day humans would walk on it? It is little wonder that a European spacecraft launched in July 2023 was called what it was: Euclid.

CONCLUSION

And so now I take my leave – but as we have seen, one cannot ever truly take one's leave from the Ancient Greeks. From philosophers like Plato, great generals like Alexander, playwrights like Aeschylus, healers like Agnodice, mathematicians like Euclid, and poets like Sappho, the achievements of the great and the good of Ancient Greece will nourish us forever.

But what is perhaps unique to the Ancient Greeks is the way that culture, for perhaps the first time, was a community activity. The people worked to bring a new way of living to fruition. There were big gaps in who could be a citizen, but the framework put in place by the Greeks remains in place to this day in a large number of nations, especially in the West. Wherever there is the city, wherever there is the rule of law, wherever there is democracy, there is Ancient Greece.

When that man from Halicarnassus, Herodotus, took up his pen, the Greek empire was in its youth. He could not have imagined that, a century later, under Alexander, it would encompass much of the known world. Nor could he have imagined that thousands of years later we would still be writing about it, talking about it, and not only thinking about it, but with it.

Herodotus may have written that "The gods love to punish whatever is greater than the rest", but it seems that when it comes to Greek culture, he was wrong...

FURTHER READING

BOOKS FROM THE TIME

Aristotle, *Politics*
Aeschylus, *The Complete Aeschylus*
Herodotus, *The Histories*
Homer, *The Iliad* and *The Odyssey*
Plato, *The Republic*
Sappho, *If Not, Winter: Fragments of Sappho* (translated by Anne Carson)
Thucydides, *History of the Peloponnesian War*

CONTEMPORARY BOOKS

Cartledge, Paul *Democracy: A Life* (2016, Oxford University Press)
Graves, Robert *The Greek Myths* (2017, Penguin)
Ober, Josiah *The Rise and Fall of Classical Greece* (2016, Princeton University Press)
Taplin, Oliver *Greek Fire: The Influence of Ancient Greece on the Modern World* (1990, Atheneum Books for Young Readers)
Waterfield, Robin *Creators, Conquerors, and Citizens* (2018, Oxford University Press)

FILMS

Jason and the Argonauts (1963), directed by Don Chaffey

Medea (1969), directed by Pier Paolo Pasolini

Iphigenia (1977), directed by Mihalis Kakogiannis

Troy (2004), directed by Wolfgang Petersen

300 (2006), directed by Zack Snyder

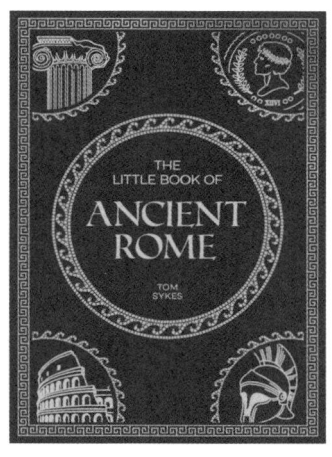

THE LITTLE BOOK OF ANCIENT ROME
Tom Sykes

Paperback • 978-1-83799-561-5

Growing from humble origins into a world-spanning empire, the Ancient Roman civilization has captured human imagination for generations. Uncover its history, from the legendary Roman army and its conquests to the art, culture and everyday life of its citizens, in this fascinating little book, which will be your pocket-sized window into the past.

Have you enjoyed this book?
If so, find us on Facebook at
Summersdale Publishers,
on Twitter/X at **@Summersdale**
and on Instagram and TikTok at
@summersdalebooks and get in touch.
We'd love to hear from you!

WWW.SUMMERSDALE.COM

Image Credits